A 33

D0304057

532 305

Advanced Introduction to Post Keynesian Economics

Elgar Advanced Introductions are stimulating and thoughtful introductions to major fields in the social sciences and law, expertly written by the world's leading scholars. Designed to be accessible yet rigorous, they offer concise and lucid surveys of the substantive and policy issues associated with discrete subject areas.

The aims of the series are two-fold: to pinpoint essential principles of a particular field, and to offer insights that stimulate critical thinking. By distilling the vast and often technical corpus of information on the subject into a concise and meaningful form, the books serve as accessible introductions for undergraduate and graduate students coming to the subject for the first time. Importantly, they also develop well-informed, nuanced critiques of the field that will challenge and extend the understanding of advanced students, scholars and policy-makers.

Titles in the series include:

International Political Economy
Benjamin J. Cohen

International Conflict and Security Law
Nigel D. White

The Austrian School of Economics
Randall G. Holcombe

Comparative Constitutional Law
Mark Tushnet

Cultural Economics
Ruth Towse

International Human Rights Law
Dinah L. Shelton

Law and Development
Michael J. Trebilcock and Mariana Mota Prado

Entrepreneurship
Robert D. Hisrich

International Humanitarian Law
Robert Kolb

International Trade Law
Michael J. Trebilcock

International Tax Law
Reuven S. Avi-Yonah

Public Policy
B. Guy Peters

Post Keynesian Economics
J.E. King

Advanced Introduction to

Post Keynesian Economics

J.E. KING

Emeritus Professor, La Trobe University, Australia and Honorary Professor, Federation University Australia

Elgar Advanced Introductions

Edward Elgar
PUBLISHING

Cheltenham, UK • Northampton, MA, USA

Published by
Edward Elgar Publishing Limited
The Lypiatts
15 Lansdown Road
Cheltenham
Glos GL50 2JA
UK

Edward Elgar Publishing, Inc.
William Pratt House
9 Dewey Court
Northampton
Massachusetts 01060
USA

A catalogue record for this book
is available from the British Library

Library of Congress Control Number: 2015933449

MIX
Paper from
responsible sources
FSC
www.fsc.org   FSC® C013056

ISBN 978 1 78254 842 3 (cased)
ISBN 978 1 78254 843 0 (paperback)
ISBN 978 1 78254 844 7 (eBook)

Typeset by Servis Filmsetting Ltd, Stockport, Cheshire
Printed and bound in Great Britain by T.J. International Ltd, Padstow

This one is for Mary

Contents

Acknowledgements

My biggest debt is to the 111 contributors to the second edition of the *Elgar Companion to Post Keynesian Economics* that I edited for publication in 2012, by whom I have been taught a very great deal about every aspect of the subject. I have also benefited from the penetrating questions asked by students at the 3rd International Summer School of the Research Network Macroeconomics and Macroeconomic Policies in Berlin in August 2011, and at the conference on The Economy in Crisis and the Crisis in Economics at the Chamber of Labour in Vienna in September 2013. Most recently, in 2014, I have learned a lot from presentations at three conferences: my own retirement conference, hosted by Federation University Australia and Victoria University; the 25th anniversary conference of the *Review of Political Economy* in Great Malvern; and the 13th conference of the Society of Heterodox Economists in Sydney. I am very grateful to the organizers of these conferences, Jerry Courvisanos and James Doughney, Stephen Parsons, and Peter Kriesler, for all their highly productive labour.

1   Introduction

Post Keynesian economics may be defined as a dissident school in macroeconomics based on a particular interpretation of John Maynard Keynes's *General Theory* (and, for some Post Keynesians, the contemporary work of the Polish economist Michał Kalecki). There is also a substantial body of work in Post Keynesian microeconomics, and some distinctive and controversial policy propositions.

I begin by setting out the core of Post Keynesian macroeconomics in Chapter 2, using the six fundamental theoretical principles asserted 20 years ago by A.P. Thirlwall and drawing some important conclusions from them. I distinguish three schools within Post Keynesian theory: the fundamentalist Keynesian approach taken by Paul Davidson; the Kaleckian variant represented by Malcolm Sawyer and Eckhard Hein; and Hyman Minsky's financial instability hypothesis. I take note of both their differences and their very extensive points of agreement, and suggest that a Kalecki–Minsky synthesis might prove an attractive option.

In Chapter 3 I show what Post Keynesian macroeconomics is *not*, outlining some very substantial criticisms of both "Old Keynesian" and "New Keynesian" ideas, Monetarism and New Classical economics, together with the New Neoclassical Synthesis that constitutes a synthesis of the latter with New Keynesian theory. These criticisms have a long history. I sketch the development of Post Keynesian theory in Cambridge (UK) and the United States in the 1950s and 1960s, describe its international dissemination in the 1970s and 1980s and conclude by summarizing the loose institutional and organization arrangements that bring Post Keynesians together in 2015.

Chapter 4 is devoted to some of the methodological issues that distinguish Post Keynesianism from the mainstream, beginning with the fundamental ontological question about the nature of the economic universe, "open system" thinking and the implications for the use of mathematical modelling and econometric research methods. I outline the Post Keynesian position(s) on the need for pluralism in economic theory and argue against the requirement that macroeconomics be provided with rigorous "microfoundations".

Then in Chapter 5 I turn to Post Keynesian microeconomics, beginning with the analysis of the firm's pricing and investment decisions and then moving to the distinctive Post Keynesian approach to the labour market. Next I consider the theory of household behaviour, which involves an approach to the theory of consumer demand, gender and labour supply that is very different from that of the mainstream. The chapter concludes with a brief outline of Post Keynesian welfare economics and its verdict on the operation of the capitalist market mechanism.

Chapter 6 deals with long-term and global questions of growth, development and the world economy. I begin by explaining how the early Cambridge Post Keynesians built on the Harrod growth model in their attempt to "generalize the *General Theory*" to the long period, and how endogenous technical change and balance of payments constraints have supplemented and enriched the basic demand-driven models of growth. The chapter concludes with a survey of Post Keynesian thinking on international economics, including trade theory, balance of payments adjustment and global capital flows.

In Chapter 7 I explain why it all matters. Here I discuss the Post Keynesian position on questions of economic policy, focussing on monetary and fiscal policy, the regulation of prices and incomes and the reform of the international monetary system. This includes strong criticism of the mainstream positions on monetary policy and on the need for fiscal austerity, together with support for a wages policy that avoids both inflation and also (possibly more relevant to the present day) deflation. I outline the Post Keynesian position on questions of international monetary reform and on some neglected macroeconomic questions of environmental policy.

In Chapter 8 I apply these principles to the Global Financial Crisis that began in 2007, beginning with the Post Keynesian analysis of the post-1970 financialization of the world economy and its consequences, and continuing with an assessment of the deregulation process that was inspired by neoliberal economic thought. I then outline the events of 2007–08, asking whether the crisis was indeed a "Minsky moment".

The chapter concludes with a discussion of the lessons that should be drawn from the crisis, drawing on the extensive Post Keynesian literature on the policy changes, national and international, that are required in order to make similar crises less likely in the future.

Chapter 9 examines the relationship between Post Keynesianism and nine other schools of heterodox economic theory: Marxian political economy; Sraffian economics; institutionalism; evolutionary economics; feminist economics; ecological economics; behavioural economics; complexity theory; and Austrian economics (of the liberal, Hayek–von Mises variety). I conclude, in the brief Chapter 10, by speculating on the future of the Post Keynesian school in an increasingly hostile organizational and intellectual climate.

Finally, a note on terminology: there are four ways of writing "Post Keynesian", with or without a hyphen, with or without a capital "p". Grammarians would almost certainly choose "post-Keynesian", but this was rejected by the founding co-editors of the *Journal of Post Keynesian Economics* because of its association with the Old Keynesian ideas that they opposed (and it is still occasionally used, rather confusingly, in a chronological rather than doctrinal sense, to refer to macroeconomic ideas developed after 1936). In this book I have followed their lead, using the "Post Keynesian" specification throughout, though I suspect that my grammar school English teachers would not have approved of this decision.

2 The core of Post Keynesian economics

Six core propositions

A.P. Thirlwall (1993) summarized Post Keynesian economics in terms of six core propositions. First, employment and unemployment are determined in the product market, not the labour market. Two major presumptions lie behind this seemingly innocuous statement, and they need to be made explicit: unemployment is a major theoretical and socio-political problem, and it is also a macroeconomic problem that cannot be reduced to microeconomics, even though it does have a microeconomic dimension. The first presumption was blindingly obvious in the mid 1930s, when Keynes was writing the *General Theory*, and it is almost as obvious in many parts of the eurozone in late 2014, but you would not know it from one recent graduate textbook, published by Princeton University Press, where neither employment nor unemployment plays any significant role. Since "including labor caused only minor changes to the previous results", Michael Wickens writes, "we shall also exclude labor where appropriate and feasible" (Wickens 2008, p. 83). This proves to be almost always, and there is no entry in the index for "unemployment" (this astonishing omission was apparently rectified in the second edition). The second presumption was universally made in the Old Keynesian literature of the 1950s and 1960s, when the distinction between demand-deficient and non-demand-deficient (or frictional and structural) unemployment was commonplace (see, for example, Perlman 1969, part 3), but you would be hard pressed to find it in mainstream textbooks today. Post Keynesians, in contrast, insist on the distinction between the microeconomic and the macroeconomic dimensions of the unemployment problem and focus their attention on the latter.

Note that Thirlwall's reference to "the product market" is not to be taken literally, for there is no such place (or social institution), only a very large number of markets for individual goods and services. It is a metaphor – one of very many that are used in economics – for the sum of expenditure on goods and services as a whole, which is what determines aggregate employment and unemployment. An income–expenditure model of some sort underpins the Post Keynesian theory of employment and unemployment, which thus relies on what is sometimes described disparagingly as "hydraulic Keynesianism", and it has done almost from the beginning of the Keynesian era (Schneider 2010, pp. 337–41). Admittedly this representation of the "circular flow" of income and expenditure is only a first step in the process of developing a more complicated and hence more satisfactory macroeconomic model (Davidson 2011, pp. 49–53), but none the less it is an essential one. Without it the Keynesian multiplier makes no sense, and the effects on income and employment of changes in investment, government spending and net exports cannot be understood.

Second, involuntary unemployment exists, and it is caused by deficient effective demand. It is not the result of labour market imperfections, and it would not be eliminated even if such imperfections were removed. This follows directly from Thirlwall's first proposition that, as we have seen, rests on the distinction between demand-deficient and non-demand-deficient unemployment. It is important to be clear on this. Post Keynesians do not deny the existence of frictional and structural unemployment, and (as will be seen in Chapter 5) they have some interesting things to say about the microeconomics of labour markets and the implications of their universal and inevitable imperfections. But the "all or nothing" fallacy must be avoided: although demand deficiency is not the only cause of unemployment, this does not imply that there is no such thing. In periods of full employment, demand-deficient unemployment is (by definition) zero, but this is the exception rather than the rule, and it has been since the end of the postwar "golden age" of capitalism in the early 1970s. Again, this was almost universally accepted half a century ago, but it is now routinely denied, or simply ignored. I remember attending a seminar presentation some years ago by a distinguished econometrician who had recently been appointed to the board of the Reserve Bank of Australia. When a colleague asked him about the link between monetary policy and unemployment, he looked puzzled. "Not our department", he replied. "That's a problem for the labour market policymakers". This not only reflected ignorance of the 1959 Act that established the Reserve Bank (which required it to take account of employment and growth in addition to inflation), but also involved a tacit denial of Thirlwall's second proposition. Post Keynesians strongly disagree.

Third, the relationship between aggregate investment and aggregate saving is fundamental to macroeconomic theory, and causation runs from investment to saving, and not vice versa. As James Meade once put it, the "Keynesian Revolution" involved a mental shift, from the picture of a dog called "saving" that wags its tail called "investment", to one of a dog called "investment" that wags its tail called "saving" (Meade 1975, p.82). We are dealing with a capitalist economy, in which the really important decisions are made by corporations, not by households or individual consumers. It is investment spending that drives the simple income–expenditure model, if we abstract (as a first simplification) from government spending and net exports. Thus it is the level of investment spending that is the independent variable determining aggregate employment, output and income, with consumption spending (and hence saving as the difference between income and expenditure) as the dependent variable, rising and falling with increases and decreases in income. This is not to say that current income is the only determinant of consumer spending, or that consumers respond passively to changes in macroeconomic circumstances. But it is investment that drives a capitalist economy, so that the theoretical analysis of such an economy must begin with the determinants of investment and not (as Wickens does) with the lifetime utility-maximizing behaviour of individual consumers. And investment is motivated by the anticipation of profit, so that the starting point of any realistic macroeconomic theory must be companies' expectations of future profitability.

Fourth, a monetary economy is quite different from a barter economy. Since profit is defined as the difference between two sums of money (revenues and costs), this should be too obvious to require much discussion, but the general equilibrium models used by mainstream macroeconomists have great difficulty in making any sense of it. It is difficult to over-estimate the importance of this point. In an early draft of the *General Theory*, Keynes used Karl Marx's representation of the capitalist circulation process to explain why money matters (Rotheim 1981), and it is unfortunate that he did not include it in the final version of the book. It is summarized in the formula $M - C - C' - M'$. The capitalist, Marx tells us, begins with a sum of money M; uses it to buy commodities (labour power and means of production) of equal value C; uses these commodities in the process of production to produce different commodities of greater value, C'; and expects to sell these commodities for a sum of money equal to this greater value, M'. The object of the exercise is to generate profit (a sum of money equal to $M' - M$, which is in turn equal to $C' - C$). If the capitalist does not expect the process to be profitable, he will not commence it, and will hold on to the original sum of money M instead. In rather old-fashioned but suitably graphic language, money can be "hoarded". Keynes coined a new term for the same phenomenon: "liquidity preference".

In this respect a capitalist economy is very different from a barter economy, where there is no money, and products are exchanged directly for other products (bread for shoes, shoes for bread). It is also very different from what Marx described as "simple" or "petty" commodity production, a classless economy of small producers whose goal is not profit but the acquisition of money from the sale of the goods that they have produced in order to purchase different commodities of equal value. This is summarized in Marx's formula $C - M - C$, but this (as Keynes puts it in a slightly different context) does not represent "the economic society in which we actually live" (Keynes 1936, p. 3). In a barter economy there is nothing (other than shoes and bread) to be hoarded, and no obvious reason to hoard them; in simple commodity production money can be hoarded, but again there is no reason to do so. In a capitalist economy, however, when profit expectations collapse there is every reason.

From this three important conclusions follow. Money is not "neutral", and macroeconomic theory cannot be partitioned into "real" and "monetary" segments, with an iron curtain separating them. Finance is important, since investment projects require expenditures in advance of the expected profit flows. Debt matters, since there is a crucial asymmetry between debtors, who can be forced to reduce their expenditure, and creditors, who cannot be forced to increase theirs. These conclusions reinforce the Post Keynesian argument that a monetary economy cannot be analysed "as if" it were a barter economy, with money introduced at a later stage like the cheese course at a banquet.

Fifth, the Quantity Theory of Money is seriously misleading, since it rests on the assumption that money is indeed neutral with respect to the determination of real output (and employment), and affects only the price level. This is the celebrated "classical dichotomy", which can be traced back at least two centuries to the work of Jean-Baptiste Say and David Ricardo. In the classical Equation of Exchange, usually written as $MV = PT$, M represents the stock of money; V is the velocity of circulation; P is the price level; and T is the volume of turnover (a proxy for real output). Assume that T is determined by "real" (that is, non-monetary) factors, above all by individual preferences for present and future consumption. Then, if V is constant, the Quantity Theory tells us that changes in M lead directly to changes in P, and only to changes in P. Changes in the stock of money lead to changes in the price level, but they do not affect output or employment, and we must make a strict distinction between the real and the monetary sectors of the economy.

Keynes rejected the classical dichotomy, and with it both the neutrality of money and the Quantity Theory itself. Post Keynesians suggest that he might have gone further, recognizing that money is endogenous to the system rather than exogenous, so that in the Equation of Exchange causation runs from right to left (from PT to MV), not from left to right (from MV to PT). In a world of credit money, where bank advances create bank deposits, the stock of money is demand-driven, so that "it is the fluctuation in the economy that causes the fluctuations in the money supply (and not the other way round)" (Kaldor 1970, p. 19). Thus "in the case of credit money the proper representation should be a *horizontal* 'supply curve' of money not a vertical one. Monetary policy is represented *not* by a given quantity of money stock but by a *given rate of interest*; and the amount of money in existence will be demand-determined" (Kaldor, 1982, p. 24, emphases in the original). In the Post Keynesian theory of inflation, increases in M are treated as the effect of inflation, not the cause. Cost-push forces are identified (especially upward pressure on wages and primary product prices) that generate inflation, often well before full employment is attained. Hence there is a need for prices and incomes policies.

Sixth, capitalist economies are driven by the "animal spirits" of investors, which determine investment decisions, rather than by precise calculations of future costs and revenues. Like many human activities, decisions to invest depend on "spontaneous optimism rather than a mathematical expectation" of profit (Keynes 1936, p. 161). Given fundamental uncertainty, it is not possible to form such expectations, even probabilistically. As Keynes later explained:

> The sense in which I am using the term [uncertainty] is that in which the prospect of a European war is uncertain, or the price of copper and the rate of interest twenty years hence, or the obsolescence of a new invention, or the position of private wealth holders in the social system in 1970. About these matters there is no scientific basis on which to form any calculable probability whatever. We simply do not know. (Keynes 1937, p. 214)

This does not mean that for Keynes investment decisions are dominated by "non-economic motives and irrational behavior", giving rise
to incessant "manias and panics", as some commentators who really
should know better have been inclined to argue (Akerlof and Shiller
2009, pp. ix–x). On the contrary: "We should not conclude from this
that everything depends on waves of irrational psychology" (Keynes
1936, p. 162). For most of the time most investors are content to apply
rather conservative conventions and rules of thumb. Manias and
panics do occur, but not often, and exactly what triggers them is itself a
complicated and contentious question.

The implications of Thirlwall's six propositions are, however, very clear,
and there are also clear implications for macroeconomic policy. The
bottom line is the "principle of effective demand". Aggregate output
and employment are often (perhaps normally) demand-constrained,
not supply-constrained. Thus Say's Law is false, and the achievement
and maintenance of full employment often (perhaps normally) requires
state intervention. Fiscal policy is not necessarily ineffective, and the
principle of "Ricardian equivalence" is false (as Ricardo himself recognized). Monetary policy cannot be restricted to a counter-inflationary
role, as the eminent Australian econometrician inferred, since it also
has real effects. Prices and incomes policies are needed to control inflation and (increasingly) to prevent deflation. Debt does matter, so that
a falling price level must be seen as part of the problem, not part of
the solution. These policy issues will be explored in greater depth in
Chapter 7.

The "fundamentalist Keynesians"

While all Post Keynesians would agree with Thirlwall's core, the
detailed exposition and elaboration of these fundamental principles
differs significantly between (at least) three distinct schools. First,
there are the "fundamentalist Keynesians", who maintain that "it's
all in the *General Theory*", as would be evident if only Keynes's mas-
terpiece were properly understood. Representatives of this school
include Victoria Chick (1983), Mark Hayes (2006) and, above all, Paul
Davidson, whose position has not changed appreciably in almost half a
century (cf. Davidson 1972 and 2011). According to Davidson, Keynes
identified the three crucial axioms of "classical" theory: ergodicity
(the future can be reliably inferred from the past); gross substitution
(price flexibility ensures that all markets clear); and the neutrality of

money (the classical dichotomy: money affects prices, not output and employment, which depend only on the "real" factors of tastes and technology).

Davidson emphasizes that Keynes believed all three axioms to be wrong. The existence of fundamental uncertainty means that we live in a non-ergodic world, in which the future cannot be reliably inferred from the past. The axiom of gross substitution is false, so that price flexibility does not guarantee full employment. And money is not neutral; it affects output and employment. From this Keynes derived the principle of effective demand, summarized in Davidson's Aggregate Supply–Aggregate Demand diagram, which was described (but not drawn) in the *General Theory*. It is quite different from the mainstream textbook version, which is drawn in price level-real GDP or inflation-real GDP space. In contrast, in Davidson's version, the vertical axis measures expected sales proceeds and planned spending, while the level of employment is measured on the horizontal axis. The intersection of the aggregate demand (*D*) and aggregate supply (*S*) curves gives the point of effective demand, which determines the level of employment; this is less than the full employment level (Davidson 2011, p. 30, figure 2.5). The corresponding equilibrium in the labour market is shown in a diagram that comes (unaccountably) almost two hundred pages later (p. 216, figure 12.5). Here the level of employment is determined in the product market – that is to say, by aggregate demand and supply – and is again less than the full employment level. Competition between employers sets the real wage above the level that would prevail at full employment, but the principle of effective demand tells us that a reduction in the real wage would not increase employment, which is determined in the product market, not in the labour market.

These diagrams reveal the nature of Davidson's microeconomics, which, as with Keynes, is essentially neoclassical (or, as Davidson would insist, Marshallian). Thus his labour demand curve slopes downwards, his labour supply curve slopes upwards, and it is implicitly assumed that the labour market is perfectly competitive; as is well known, under monopsony there *is* no labour demand curve. Davidson is a strong critic of what he describes as "imperfectionism". The principle of effective demand, he insists, has nothing to do with imperfections in the labour market or the product market, and eliminating such imperfections, even if it were possible, would not reduce demand-deficient unemployment. Like Keynes, Davidson argues that the principle of effective demand demonstrates the need for active monetary, fiscal and incomes policies. He also advocates the reform of the international monetary system along the lines advocated by Keynes in 1944 with his proposal for an International Clearing Union (see Davidson 2009 for an eloquent summary of his views on macroeconomic policy).

The Kaleckians

The Polish economist Michał Kalecki discovered the principle of effective demand more or less simultaneously with Keynes, but gave it a Marxist twist that emphasized the class nature of capitalist society (Toporowski 2013). Kaleckian models are used by many Post Keynesians, especially in Europe, where Malcolm Sawyer (1985) and Eckhard Hein (2014) have been especially influential (see also Hein and Stockhammer 2011). The distinction between workers and capitalists is implicit in the *General Theory*, but Keynes does not pay it the attention that it deserves. For Kalecki it is absolutely essential, since capitalist expenditure (above all on investment) is the key to the business cycle. He draws a clear distinction between the savings propensities of capitalists and workers, which leads him to the famous aphorism (which accurately reflects his views, but which no one has been able to locate in his published work) that "workers spend what they get; capitalists get what they spend".

Kalecki's algebra is derived from the simplest income–expenditure model, and reveals that in a closed economy with no government, total profits are indeed equal to capitalists' expenditure (in a more complicated and realistic model, we must add the government deficit and the trade surplus). Write Y for total income; C for consumption (the suffixes w and p refer respectively to consumption spending by workers and capitalists, out of their wage and profit incomes); I for investment; W for total wages; and P for total profits. In the simplest case, with no government or overseas sector,

$$\text{Total Expenditure} = C + I = C_w + C_p + I,$$

and

$$\text{Total Income} = W + P.$$

Assuming that there is no saving by workers, so that $C_w = W$, equality of income and expenditure entails that

$$P = C_p + I.$$

Here causation runs from expenditure to income, that is, from right to left. Thus, in aggregate, profits are determined by capitalists' expenditure on consumption and on investment (especially on the latter, since it depends on expected profits and is therefore much more volatile than consumption spending).

Now add the government, which incurs expenditure (G) and collects tax revenue (T). It follows that

$$\text{Total Expenditure } Y = C + I + G = C_w + C_p + I + G,$$

while

$$\text{Total Income } Y = W + P + T.$$

Again assume no saving by workers. Once again $C_w = W$, so that

$$P = (C_p + I) + (G - T),$$

and total profits are now equal to expenditure by capitalists plus the budget deficit.

Finally allow for an open economy, which means adding spending on exports by foreigners (X) to total expenditure and spending by locals on imports (M) to the uses that are made of total income. It is easy to show that

$$P = (C_p + I) + (G - T) + (X - M),$$

so that aggregate profits now depend on expenditure by capitalists plus the budget deficit plus the trade surplus. Adding saving (or dis-saving) by workers makes the algebra a little more complicated, but does not affect the thrust of the argument.

The distribution of income between capital and labour plays a more important role in the Kaleckian macroeconomic model than it does for the fundamentalist Keynesians, so that the determination of relative shares is a central problem (Kalecki 1954 [1991]). For Kalecki the profit share depends on the degree of monopoly in oligopolistic product markets (and also, in his later work, on the outcome of class conflict in the labour market). Fluctuations in investment expenditure are the key to the business cycle, but there is also a tendency for a chronic deficiency in effective demand, as suggested by early underconsumptionists like Rosa Luxemburg, since the profit share is normally too high, and the wage share too low, to generate enough consumption expenditure to sustain full employment of labour or capital. But this is a capitalist society, and the ruling class will normally resist government deficit spending, even though it would increase total profits. In part this reflects a mistaken belief in the need for "sound finance", in part a well-founded fear of full employment as a threat to "discipline in the factories" (Kalecki 1943 [1990]). Armaments expenditure is less objectionable to the capitalists than civilian spending, however, so that "Military Keynesianism" may prove politically acceptable where high wages and the welfare state are not. In the late 1960s, almost at the end of his life, Kalecki came to accept that after 1945 capitalism had undergone a "crucial reform", in which real wages had risen and state welfare spending had supplemented military expenditure and allowed the maintenance of full employment. But he argued – correctly, as subsequent events have shown – that this was a fragile and probably also a temporary achievement (King 2013).

Hyman Minsky and the financial instability hypothesis

The "Wall Street vision" of capitalism articulated by Hyman Minsky was rather different from Kalecki's, but not fundamentally inconsistent with it. The central relationship that interested Minsky was not that between the capitalist employer and the worker, but rather that between the investment banker and his capitalist client. Minsky's "representative agent" is neither a classless consumer (as in mainstream economic theory) nor an industrial capitalist (as for Marx and Kalecki), but a financial capitalist. Borrowing and lending are the crucial transactions, not buying consumer goods or labour power. Minsky's agents are "representative", or herd-like, only at certain stages of the business cycle: they emulate each other in the upswing, when they are all equally exuberant, and also in the downswing, when they are cautious or distinctly pessimistic. But the behaviour of atypical or non-representative agents is important at the critical turning points. At the start of a boom, someone has to have the confidence to borrow, and to lend, on a greatly increased scale. At the beginning of a financial crisis, someone has to lose faith in their clients' creditworthiness and call in their loans.

Since capitalism is inescapably cyclical (and not prone to stagnation, Minsky always insisted), fluctuations in investment are crucial, and the availability of finance is central to investment. Lending standards fluctuate over the cycle. As is well known, Minsky distinguished three phases: "hedge finance" in the early stages of an upswing, when lenders accommodate only those borrowers whose projects are expected to be sufficiently profitable to allow them to make both the necessary interest payments and repay the principal; "speculative finance", where lenders are less cautious, and no longer require that the repayment of the principal is guaranteed, only the interest; and "Ponzi finance", where lending standards become so lax that some borrowers need to take out further loans in order to meet their interest obligations (the 2008 case of the US swindler Bernie Madoff was uncannily similar to that of the eponymous Charles Ponzi almost a century earlier). The eventual, inevitable financial crisis results from a collapse in lenders' confidence and leads to credit rationing, the forced liquidation of assets at "fire sale" prices in order to repay loans, a sharp fall in investment and a consequent decline in output and employment (Minsky 1986 [2008]).

There is no suggestion in Minsky's work that fluctuations in output and employment are caused by the decisions of the monetary authorities. Instead he saw the business cycle as the result of endogenous monetary instability, which results from the behaviour of financial agents in the private sector. Government policy is not part of the problem but instead the most important part of the solution. Unlike many Marxists (and not a few Keynesians), Minsky was emphatically not a stagnationist. He saw capitalism as essentially dynamic – not least in its capacity for financial innovation – but also (and in consequence) as inherently unstable. But capitalism cannot be understood, or successfully modelled, in "real" terms, neglecting the central role of money and finance as the supposedly "Keynesian" growth and trade cycle models of the 1940s and 1950s had attempted to do.

Late in his life Minsky identified a new stage in the development of the financial sector, which he termed "money manager capitalism", in which consumer borrowing, and hence also consumer debt, had become more important (Minsky 1987 [2008]). Under money manager capitalism, new financial instruments traded by new institutions in new markets were continually eroding the banks' share of assets and liabilities, forcing them into more and more risky forms of behaviour. Minsky did not live to see the rise of "shadow banking" in the United

States in the early years of the twentieth-first century, but he would not have been surprised by its ability to evade almost all regulation by the monetary authorities (Gabor 2014).

As a student of Joseph Schumpeter, Minsky always emphasized the crucial role of financial innovation in all stages of capitalist development. This meant that there was a constant need for close financial regulation, and also a constant threat that it would be ineffective. Why, then, had a financial crisis on the scale of the Great Depression not happened again in Minsky's lifetime (he died in 1996)? "Big Government" was the answer, he believed. There was both a flow dimension and a stock dimension to this. In the post-1945 United States the government was much larger than it had been in 1929, which made built-in fiscal stabilizers much more powerful in a downturn; this was the flow aspect. In addition, the sum of all the budget deficits since 1929 had provided the private sector with a huge quantity of risk-free government securities, greatly improving its financial robustness; this was the stock aspect. But eternal vigilance remained the price of continuing financial stability.

One school or three?

Evidently these three Post Keynesian schools occupy a very considerable area of common ground. In particular, they all agree that it is impossible to base macroeconomic theory on RARE "microfoundations" (where the acronym denotes representative agents with rational expectations). Rational expectations are ruled out for Davidson by non-ergodicity and fundamental Keynesian uncertainty, and for Minsky by the cyclical myopia of his investment bankers; Kalecki, too, stresses the importance of irreducible "borrowers' risk" and "lenders' risk". Neither is there any role for representative agents, since this would eliminate the bulls and bears who are central to Keynes and Davidson, the workers and capitalists who are emphasized by Kalecki, and the debtors and creditors who are distinguished by Minsky. At least two classes of agents are always involved, in any Post Keynesian macroeconomic model, and they cannot behave "rationally" in the strict neoclassical sense, since they lack the necessary information (which is not to say, Keynes stressed, that they do not normally act in a reasonable manner).

It should also be noted that Kalecki and Minsky need each other. In Kalecki's models there is no substantial role for money or finance. It is not that he believed that capitalism could be analysed as if it were a barter economy, but simply that he chose to concentrate on other questions. Kalecki was not a great reader, and it is entirely possible that he knew nothing about Minsky. But the latter's emphasis on cyclical variability in credit rationing and on asset price fluctuations might well have been useful to Kalecki in resolving the continuing problems that he had in specifying an acceptable macroeconomic investment function, which were noted by his disciple Josef Steindl (1990, pp. 139–48).

As for Minsky: he needed a theory of financial resources to complement his theory of financial commitments. Capitalists obtain income in the form of the profits that are generated by their activities, and they only encounter financial difficulties if their incomes are inadequate to meet their obligations to their creditors. Kalecki's theory of profits provides a clear and coherent theory of capitalists' aggregate financial resources, as Minsky himself came to recognize rather late in his career. And this points to a problem for him: since total profits are determined by the sum of investment and capitalist consumption expenditure, it is entirely possible that capitalists can spend their way out of trouble, in aggregate (thought not, of course, individually). Again, the investment function is the critical part of any Post Keynesian model.

References

Akerlof, G. and R. Shiller. 2009. *Animal Spirits: How Human Psychology Drives the Economy, and Why It Matters for Global Capitalism*, Princeton, NJ: Princeton University Press.

Chick, V. 1983. *Macroeconomics after Keynes*, Oxford: Philip Allan.

Davidson, P. 1972. *Money and the Real World*, London: Macmillan.

Davidson, P. 2009. *The Keynes Solution: The Path to Global Economic Prosperity*, Basingstoke: Palgrave Macmillan.

Davidson, P. 2011. *Post Keynesian Macroeconomic Theory: A Foundation for Successful Economic Policies for the Twenty-first Century*, second edn, Cheltenham, UK and Northampton, MA, USA: Edward Elgar.

Gabor, D. 2014. "The political economy of repo markets", Mimeo, University of Western England, Bristol.

Hayes, M.G. 2006. *The Economics of Keynes: A New Guide to the General Theory*, Cheltenham, UK and Northampton, MA, USA: Edward Elgar.

Hein, E. 2014. *Distribution and Growth after Keynes: A Post Keynesian Guide*, Cheltenham, UK and Northampton, MA, USA: Edward Elgar.

Hein, E. and E. Stockhammer (eds). 2011. *A Modern Guide to Keynesian Macroeconomics and Economic Policies*, Cheltenham, UK and Northampton, MA, USA: Edward Elgar.

THE CORE OF POST KEYNESIAN ECONOMICS

Kaldor, N. 1970. "The new monetarism", *Lloyds Bank Review*, **97**, 1–18, reprinted in N. Kaldor (1978), *Further Essays in Applied Economics*, London: Duckworth, pp. 1–21.

Kaldor, N. 1982. *The Scourge of Monetarism*, Oxford: Oxford University Press.

Kalecki, M. 1943. "Political aspects of full employment", *Political Quarterly*, **14**(4), October–December, 322–31, reprinted in J. Osiatýnski (ed.) (1990), *Collected Works of Michał Kalecki. Volume 1. Capitalism, Business Cycles and Full Employment*, Oxford: Clarendon Press. pp. 347–57.

Kalecki, M. 1954. *Theory of Economic Dynamics. An Essay on Cyclical and Long-Run Changes in Capitalist Economy*, London: Allen and Unwin, reprinted in J. Osiatýnski (ed.) (1991), *Collected Works of Michał Kalecki. Volume 2. Capitalism, Economic Dynamics*, Oxford: Clarendon Press, pp. 205–348.

Keynes, J.M. 1936. *The General Theory of Employment, Interest and Money*, London: Macmillan.

Keynes, J.M. 1937. "The general theory of employment", *Quarterly Journal of Economics*, **51**(2), February, 209–23.

King, J.E. 2013. "Whatever happened to the crucial reform?", in R. Bellofiore, E. Karwowski and J. Toporowski (eds), *Economic Crisis and Political Economy: Volume 2 of Essays in Honour of Tadeusz Kowalik*, Basingstoke: Palgrave Macmillan, pp. 29–41.

Meade, J.E. 1975. "The Keynesian revolution", in M. Keynes (ed.), *Essays on John Maynard Keynes*, Cambridge: Cambridge University Press, pp. 82–8.

Minsky, H.P. 1986. *Stabilizing an Unstable Economy*, New Haven, CT: Yale University Press, second edition 2008, New York: McGraw-Hill.

Minsky, H.P. 1987. "Securitization", Policy Note 2008/2, Levy Economics Institute of Bard College, Annadale-on-Hudson, NY.

Perlman, R. 1969. *Labor Theory*, New York: Wiley.

Rotheim, R. 1981. "Keynes's monetary theory of value (1933)", *Journal of Post Keynesian Economics*, **3**(4), Summer, 568–85.

Sawyer, M. 1985. *The Economics of Michał Kalecki*, Basingstoke: Macmillan.

Schneider, M.P. 2010. "Keynesian income determination diagrams", in M. Blaug and P. Lloyd (eds), *Famous Figures and Diagrams in Economics*, Cheltenham, UK and Northampton, MA, USA: Edward Elgar, pp. 337–47.

Steindl, J. 1990. *Economic Papers 1941–88*, Basingstoke: Macmillan.

Thirlwall, A.P. 1993. "The renaissance of Keynesian economics", *Banca Nazionale del Lavoro Quarterly Review*, **186**, September, 327–37.

Toporowski, J. 2013. *Michał Kalecki. Volume 1, Rendezvous in Cambridge, 1899–1939*, Basingstoke: Palgrave Macmillan.

Wickens, M. 2008. *Macroeconomic Theory: A Dynamic General Equilibrium Approach*, Princeton, NJ: Princeton University Press.

3 What Post Keynesian macroeconomics is *not*

Pre-Keynesian macroeconomics

The name of John Maynard Keynes has all too often been taken in vain by theorists with whom he would have had little or nothing in common. This is true to some extent of Old Keynesians like J.R. Hicks and Don Patinkin (as Hicks himself came to acknowledge late in life), and even more so in the case of the twenty-first-century New Keynesians. Keynes himself identified his target as "classical economics", an umbrella term that covered more than a century of macroeconomic thinking, from Say and Ricardo to Wicksell and Pigou, and thus included post-1870 neoclassical theory in addition to pre-1830 classical political economy and important intermediaries like John Stuart Mill. The two propositions that Keynes took issue with most vigorously in the work of his predecessors were Say's Law and the "natural" rate of interest. Say's Law was touched on in Chapter 2. It is best defined as the belief that, whatever the sources of macroeconomic problems might be, insufficient aggregate demand is not one of them. Thus while there can be over-production of individual commodities, there can never be a "general glut". Say's Law is thus the antithesis of Keynes's principle of effective demand.

In pre-Keynesian economics the "natural" rate of interest is the interest rate that equates the demand and supply of "loanable funds" and so brings saving and investment into equality at the full employment level of output. The classical economists often explained business cycles as the result of the actual rate of interest deviating from the natural level, giving rise first to excessive levels of saving and investment (in the boom) and then to insufficient levels (in the slump). The title of Keynes's book – *The General Theory of Employment, Interest and Money* – reveals both how important he thought this question to be, and how mistaken he believed the loanable funds theory of interest actually was. For Keynes the rate of interest equates the supply and demand for money, while savings and investment are brought into equality by changes in the level of income. The demand for money, he argued, is the result of liquidity preference: the desire for a safe store of value in a world of fundamental uncertainty, where the prices of all other assets were unpredictable.

"The composition of this book", he wrote in the "Preface" to the *General Theory*, "has been for the author a long struggle of escape ... from habitual modes of thought and expression ... which ramify, for those brought up as most of us have been, into every corner of our minds" (Keynes 1936, p. viii). He himself had no doubt that he had made a fundamental break with "classical" macroeconomics, and 11 years later – long before the appearance of Thomas Kuhn's *Structure of Scientific Revolutions* – his American disciple Lawrence Klein published a book entitled *The Keynesian Revolution* (Klein 1947).

Old Keynesian macroeconomics

Some of those attracted by the message of the *General Theory*, however, did not accept that it necessitated such a radical break with the past. Instead they claimed that Keynes's insights could be reconciled with much of the pre-1936 orthodoxy, and constructed what came to be known as the "neoclassical (or neoclassical-Keynesian) synthesis", and today often goes under the label Old Keynesian economics. By the mid 1950s it was generally regarded as the correct interpretation of Keynes's thought, by supporters and opponents alike. However, the one thing that unites Post Keynesians of all persuasions is their rejection of the principal elements of Old Keynesian theory. Indeed, Post Keynesian economics in the United States very largely arose from a critique of the Old Neoclassical Synthesis, as we shall see later in this chapter.

The first component of Old Keynesian macroeconomics is the IS-LM model. This was a multiple discovery, which seems to have met with Keynes's approval (King 2002, p. 31). But there are very serious problems with it. First, it deals with the wrong variables, and the well-known IS-LM diagram thus has the wrong axes, which should be inflation and employment, not output and the rate of interest. Second, there are good reasons for believing the IS curve to be both interest-inelastic and highly unstable, since investment depends on profit expectations (and hence on "animal spirits"), much more than on the rate of interest, and it will shift every time these expectations change. Third, as we saw in Chapter 2, the stock of money is endogenous: it is determined by the demand for credit, and this means that the LM curve is horizontal, not vertical. For all these reasons, IS-LM is a source of confusion rather than enlightenment.

The same is true of the second component of Old Keynesian macroeconomics, the Solow (or more accurately Solow–Swan) growth model, which is rejected by Post Keynesians on several grounds. First, they object to its treatment of the long run as a sort of magic kingdom where Say's Law holds, labour and capital are both always fully employed, and the principle of effective demand is therefore inapplicable. (Many would agree with Kalecki that there is no such thing as the long run, but only a series of short runs.) Second, they point to the incoherence of the neoclassical theory of capital on which the Solow growth model relies, and in particular to what Heinz Kurz has described as the "monotonic fallacy" regarding capital–labour substitution. As demonstrated by Piero Sraffa, there is no good reason to believe that a change in the ratio of the real wage to the rate of profit will always induce a change in the labour–capital ratio in the opposite direction, as the Solow model requires. This was established in the 1960s in the course of the long and acrimonious "Cambridge controversies" in the theory of capital (Harcourt 1972). Finally, there is every reason to believe that technical change is endogenous, and responds to changes in demand. As will be seen in Chapter 6, the endogeneity of technical change is an important part of Post Keynesian growth theory. It also puts Say's Law into reverse, since there is a sense in which demand creates its own supply, and lack of demand results in stunted supply (a proposition associated with the related concepts of cumulative causation, path dependence and hysteresis).

The third and final component of Old Keynesian economics is the Phillips Curve, which links the rate of wage inflation to the extent of demand deficiency in the labour market, as measured by the unemployment rate. If the relationship between wage inflation and unemployment is sufficiently stable, the Phillips Curve can be treated as a menu for policy choice, a sort of macroeconomic budget constraint on government policy, as set out in the influential paper by Samuelson and Solow (1960). Post Keynesians reject this narrowly economic analysis in favour of a multi-disciplinary or political economy approach to explaining inflation, in which political influences, labour market institutions and (especially) the class power of capital relative to labour are much more important in determining the rate at which money wages and prices increase than the unemployment rate (Arestis 1992, chapter 7; Forder 2014).

Monetarism

This also brought the Post Keynesians into conflict with the monetarists, whose influence had increased substantially with the acceleration of inflation and the emergence of stagflation in the late 1960s and early 1970s. They were no more surprised than the monetarists were by the instability that the Phillips Curve displayed in this period. But, as we have seen, they explained it in a very different fashion, arguing that heightened social conflict over the distribution of income was more important in increasing inflation than were increased inflationary expectations, and criticizing monetarism above all for its rejection of the principle of effective demand.

The most sustained and systematic attack on the monetarists came from Nicholas Kaldor (King 2009, chapter 7). Kaldor objected first and foremost to Milton Friedman's restoration of the two pre-Keynesian doctrines, the neutrality of money and the "classical dichotomy". For the monetarists, only money matters in determining "money things" (money output, the price level, the level of money wages); "other things", like fiscal policy or trade union behaviour, do not matter. Conversely, money cannot influence "real things" (output and employment), except temporarily. Since money was *not* neutral, Kaldor maintained, and the classical dichotomy was a mistake, the Quantity Theory could not be upheld. Here Kaldor became the foremost exponent of Thirlwall's fifth principle of Post Keynesian macroeconomics, outlined in Chapter 2. In the Quantity Equation, $MV = PT$, he argued, causation runs principally from right to left, not (as Friedman maintained) from left to right. And V, the velocity of circulation, was variable, not constant.

There was an important methodological dimension to Kaldor's argument, which had to do with the historical specificity of the theory of money. The monetarists had failed to recognize the implications of the move from commodity money to credit money. Unlike gold and silver, "credit money has no 'supply function' in the production sense (since its costs of production are insignificant if not actually zero); it comes into existence as a result of bank lending and is extinguished through the repayment of bank loans" (Kaldor 1982, p. 15). Hence it makes no sense to claim that inflation is caused by an "excess supply of money";

in a system of credit money, there can be no such excess supply. The stock of credit money is endogenous, being determined by the demand for loans. A more detailed version of this argument soon came from Victoria Chick (1992, chapter 12), who distinguished no less than five stages in the development of the banking system and the decline of commodity money and spelled out their implications for the theory of saving, investment and interest.

Kaldor's horizontal money supply curve, contrasted with the vertical money supply curve that was assumed by the monetarists, proved to be a very effective rhetorical device (even if it was not obviously consistent with his "in principle" denial that there could be any such supply curve). The dispute between "horizontalists and verticalists" – the title of an influential text on endogenous money by Basil Moore (1988) – centred on two major points of disagreement about monetary policy. The first, and less important, concerned the nature of the policy instrument. For the monetarists, it was the money stock, which should be restricted to grow at a constant rate equal to the trend rate of growth of real output. For the Post Keynesians, the money stock could not be controlled by the authorities, since it was endogenous (and therefore demand-determined). The velocity of circulation was also highly variable, so that neither M nor MV could be effectively controlled; thus the only available policy instrument was the rate of interest. The experience of the 1980s, when monetarist ideas dominated the macroeconomic policies of the Thatcher and Reagan administrations, demonstrated that the Post Keynesians were correct. Kaldor was also vindicated on the second (and much more significant) issue, which concerned the effects of tight monetary policy. The classical dichotomy proved to be quite wrong, with the high interest rates of the 1980s contributing – along with a substantial contractionary shift in fiscal policy – to a sharp reduction in real output and a large increase in unemployment (but only a slow decline in the inflation rate).

New Classical economics

The analytical basis of monetarism was relatively thin. Milton Friedman was no great theorist, relying more on empirical evidence– especially the supposed constancy of the velocity of circulation and consequent stability of the demand for money – than on any elaborate model of individual decision-making. Despite a throwaway reference to the Walrasian equations of general equilibrium in the most frequently quoted summary of his ideas (Friedman 1968, p. 8), he was no enthusiast for general equilibrium modelling. In fact Friedman showed no great interest in the provision of rigorous microfoundations for his macroeconomics (and indeed once acknowledged that, like Keynes, he preferred to do his economics "top down, not bottom up"). This was evident in his treatment of inflationary expectations as being "adaptive" in nature, that is, determined by the difference between the rate of inflation that economic agents had expected in the recent past and the actual course of events, rather than deriving expectations from a formal model of rational, maximizing behaviour.

The second generation of monetarists were very different. For Robert Lucas and his colleagues, macroeconomic theory had to be grounded in a rigorous general equilibrium model of the lifetime utility-maximizing decisions of RARE individuals – representative agents with rational expectations – who did not make the systematic and persistent mistakes that were entailed by Friedman-style adaptive expectations. The resulting "New Classical" theory involved some very distinctive and contentious claims (Vercelli 1991). First, financial markets are invariably efficient, in the sense that agents use all available information and therefore never make systematic mistakes. Second, business cycles always reflect equilibrium, utility-maximizing responses to "real" shocks, and thus never result in involuntary unemployment. Third, agents recognize that government budget deficits today will require higher taxation tomorrow and adjust their consumption spending accordingly, so that fiscal policy is always ineffective (this principle of "Ricardian equivalence" explains the "New Classical" tag, though David Ricardo himself did not believe it).

Post Keynesians criticized every aspect of New Classical theory, right from the start. Paul Davidson acknowledged the objections raised by Old Keynesians like James Tobin concerning the unrealistic assumptions made by Lucas, which included the simultaneous clearing of all markets and the existence of forward markets for all contingencies until the end of time. But Davidson's objections went deeper than this. The New Classical models of rational expectations relied on the assumption that the economic world was ergodic. In a non-ergodic world characterized by fundamental Keynesian uncertainty, rational decision-making cannot prevent agents from making systematic errors over time. In such a world, "the present population can learn little about future objective distribution functions from past evidence except perhaps to 'know' that they may be different from the past and present functions" (Davidson 1982–83, p. 186). In a non-ergodic world, money is held as a precaution against uncertainty, and this is sufficient to rule out the classical dichotomy and the neutrality of money.

New Keynesian macroeconomics

New Keynesian economics originated as a critique of New Classical theory, taking issue above all with the assumption of a rapid return to equilibrium in reaction to shocks. Instead the New Keynesians pointed to the widespread existence of imperfections in the markets for products and (especially) labour, so that wages and prices adjusted only slowly and continuous equilibrium could therefore not be assumed. In these circumstances both workers and firms were behaving rationally when they preferred quantity adjustments to price adjustments. In unionized labour markets, collective agreements almost always prevented firms from reducing wages during the life of the agreement, but permitted layoffs if market conditions deteriorated; this imposed a significant degree of rigidity upon the level of money wages. Even where there were no unions, the New Keynesians argued, employers were reluctant to force down wages by threatening existing workers with the loss of their jobs to lower-paid outsiders, for fear of the effects on morale and hence on productivity. "Efficiency wages", which minimized the unit labour cost of production, therefore tended to be inflexible downwards even without interference from unions.

Similarly, the New Keynesians maintained, product markets were rarely perfectly competitive. Under monopolistic competition, price rigidity reflected the importance of stable, long-term relationships between suppliers and their customers. In addition, there were significant "menu costs" that deterred frequent upward revision of price lists. Finally, asymmetric information between borrowers and lenders prevents capital markets from clearing and explains the widespread existence of credit rationing.

Post Keynesians reject this fundamental principle of New Keynesian theory, which is sometimes referred to as "imperfectionism" and which is inconsistent with the principle of effective demand. Downward wage and price flexibility would not, they assert, be sufficient to establish and maintain full employment. In fact deflation is seen by Post Keynesians as part of the problem, and not as part of the solution to involuntary unemployment. As Keynes argued at some length in chapter 19 of the *General Theory*, there was a strong case for the maintenance of a stable price and money wage level. Deflation was a very bad idea, he believed, for at least three reasons. First, expectations of further price reductions would encourage consumers to postpone expenditure, reducing effective demand. Second, the increasing real burden of debt that was fixed in money terms would increase financial fragility and discourage business investment. Finally, since it was not possible for the money rate of interest to become negative, a falling price level would increase the real rate of interest, with negative effects on both consumption and investment demand (Keynes 1936, pp. 257–71). The experience of Japan since 1990 provides a cautionary case study in the dangers of even very gradual deflation.

Thus Post Keynesians maintain that very little of New Keynesian theory is either new or Keynesian (Cornwall 2012; Davidson 2011, chapter 11). The positive relationship between wages and labour productivity has been acknowledged for many decades (if not centuries), and the importance of the perceived fairness of wage-fixing by employers had been recognized by neoclassical theorists like (the pre-Keynesian) Hicks (1932). Keynes himself had denied that involuntary unemployment was the result of imperfections in the labour market.

In fact the fundamental Post Keynesian objection to New Keynesian theory is directed to its acceptance of the false proposition that the principle of effective demand would not apply in perfectly competitive labour and product markets, with (downwardly) flexible wages and prices. In effect the New Keynesians accept the axioms of New Classical economics as the general case, or analytical starting point, merely casting doubt on their empirical relevance. The policy prescriptions that follow from this false premise are also entirely anti-Keynesian, focussing on the need for greater flexibility in product and (especially) labour markets, floating exchange rates and small government.

The defects of New Keynesianism are especially evident in its approach to monetary theory, which is simply "a recasting of the old classical dichotomy in new clothes" (Rogers 2013, p. 168). It rests on a model of general equilibrium in which there is really no role for money, since all the functions of money are performed by the Walrasian auctioneer. In effect the New Keynesians assume an ergodic world, with the postulate of "complete financial markets" (Woodford 2003, p. 64) entailing that all future eventualities can be insured against – and that those offering insurance contracts will never default on them. All this is too much for one prominent self-professed New Keynesian, Joseph Stiglitz, who insists on the dangers of deflation and the importance of combating financial fragility (Stiglitz 2010, pp. 260–1). But Stiglitz also pulls his punches, making no explicit criticism of Lucas or other New Classical theorists and being seemingly unaware of the work of Hyman Minsky.

The New Neoclassical Synthesis

The New Neoclassical Synthesis operates on three levels. First, in terms of undergraduate teaching, a simple three-equation model has replaced the old IS-LM apparatus of the original neoclassical synthesis. The first is an aggregate demand curve, making real output a negative function of the rate of interest; this is the old IS curve slightly reconfigured. The second is a downward-sloping short-run Phillips Curve, making the inflation rate a negative function of the output gap (itself closely and positively related to the unemployment rate). The novelty lies with the third equation, which replaces the LM curve and makes the real short-run interest rate a positive function of the central bank's expected inflation rate; this is the "Taylor rule" for monetary policy.

Post Keynesians can take some pleasure from the third equation, which incorporates their claims that money is endogenous and that the monetary authorities are able to control interest rates, not the stock of money. It also unwittingly acknowledges the important methodological principle that macroeconomic theory must be historically and socially specific – the Taylor rule would have been unthinkable before central bankers abandoned their monetarist illusions, and reasserted their "independence", in the late 1980s. This does not prevent the Post Keynesians from pointing out that neither function is likely to be stable over space or time, with both uncertainty and social conflict being neglected in the mainstream account. In essence, then, the teaching version of the "new consensus" model is quite similar to Old Keynesian theory.

The second level of the New Neoclassical Synthesis is the advanced theoretical analysis, with microfoundations, in which the three undergraduate relations are rigorously derived from a rational choice model of a forward-looking, utility-maximizing, classless individual agent. The canonical text is Woodford (2003), a work that combines considerable scholarship and great ingenuity with considerable detachment from capitalist reality. Post Keynesians object, first and foremost, that it is not the economic theory of a capitalist economy, in which there must be two classes of "representative agents" (workers and capitalists), not one, and capitalist profit expectations are what drive the entire system (Heilbroner and Milberg 1995). Money is thus essential, since profit is defined as the difference between two sums of money: revenues and costs. In the New Neoclassical Synthesis, however, as in all general equilibrium models in the Walrasian tradition, there is no clear role for money. Woodford is forced to treat it – bizarrely – as a friction or imperfection (Rogers 2006).

Second, the savings–investment relation, which must be central to any genuinely Keynesian analysis, is dealt with in a pre-Keynesian manner. Equilibrium between saving and investment is established when the market interest rate equals the "natural rate" of interest. For Keynes, as for the Post Keynesians, there is a different equilibrium (or "natural") rate of interest for each level of effective demand, and thus there is a different equilibrium interest rate for every level of employment. In denying this, Say's Law has been smuggled back into the New Neoclassical Synthesis. Third, the insistence on providing rigorous neoclassical microfoundations for macroeconomic theory amounts to a denial of the fallacy of composition, which Keynes regarded as the methodological pre-condition for having a separate macroeconomics in the first place. I shall have more to say on this question in Chapter 4.

Finally, the New Neoclassical Synthesis has an operational level. For econometric estimation, forecasting and policy evaluation, its practitioners use dynamic stochastic general equilibrium (DSGE) models. They are "dynamic", since they model the multi-period behaviour of rational forward-looking agents; "stochastic", since they are subjected to unexpected events, or "shocks"; and "general equilibrium", since the influence of Walrasian theory has proved more lasting among mainstream macroeconomists than it has among their microeconomist colleagues. DSGE models *appear* to have "Keynesian" features, including imperfect competition, incomplete information and price and wage rigidities.

However, Post Keynesian critics have concluded that these models are not in any true sense Keynesian, since they do not acknowledge the existence of involuntary unemployment and have no obvious role for money (Arestis 2009). In DSGE models the labour market is always in equilibrium; the level of employment varies only because households make inter-temporal consumption–leisure substitution decisions in response to unexpected (and temporary) changes in the real wage. The output gap in such models is thus an optimal reaction to these changes.

Moreover, the "transversality condition", which is required to make these models mathematically tractable, entails that no one ever defaults on their financial obligations. But, if you can always rely on a promise to pay, there is no point in asking for (or holding) cash. Hence there are no banks (and no entry for that word in the 21-page index to Woodford's book), no bank failures, no finance, no financial crises and no effective demand failures. Monetary policy operates only through changes in the rate of interest, and only affects consumption expenditure. Post Keynesians conclude that DSGE models are Real Business Cycle models in everything but name (Dullien 2011). They raise the spectre of the Trojan horse (apparently Keynesian, but with New Classical economists lurking inside). Thomas Palley (2008) uses an even more telling metaphor, describing the New Neoclassical Synthesis as "cuckoo economics": the (European) cuckoo lays its eggs in the nest of another species, leaving the unwitting host to hatch them and rear the chicks as if they were its own.

Some history

Post Keynesian theory originated in the 1950s and 1960s, more or less independently in Britain and the United States. By the early 1970s the term was being widely used to describe the ideas discussed in Chapter 2, and by the end of the decade a more or less clearly defined Post Keynesian school had emerged. The most important of the early British Post Keynesians were Joan Robinson and Nicholas Kaldor. Rather than attacking the Old Neoclassical Synthesis, their principal concern was to fill in the gaps left by Keynes, in particular to develop theories of growth and distribution that were consistent with the principle of effective demand. This did eventually lead them into conflict with the Solow growth model, especially after the Italian theorist Piero Sraffa, who had lived in Cambridge since the late 1920s, finally published his devastating attack on the coherence of neoclassical capital theory.

The main landmarks of Cambridge Post Keynesianism were Robinson's magisterial *The Accumulation of Capital* (1956), Kaldor's short but influential article on "Alternative theories of distribution" (1956) and Sraffa's slim volume, *Production of Commodities by Means of Commodities* (1960). They established a Cambridge tradition, in which the Harrod growth model was supplemented by a macroeconomic theory of distribution where the income shares of wages and profits were determined by capitalists' investment decisions and the very different propensities to save of capitalists and workers. There was no role for neoclassical production functions or for the marginal productivity theory of distribution. Kaldor later developed a range of growth models that made technical progress endogenous, and pioneered the Post Keynesian analysis of monetary endogeneity and the consequent critique of the Quantity Theory. Robinson, for her part, came to attack the Old Neoclassical Synthesis as a form of "Bastard Keynesianism", aimed at "putting Keynes to sleep". In this she may well have been influenced by the US Post Keynesian Sidney Weintraub, who had developed a very similar critique independently of the Cambridge (UK) theorists.

In addition to Sraffa, two other Italians played an important role in the development of Post Keynesian thinking in Britain. Luigi Pasinetti corrected a major defect in Kaldor's macroeconomic theory of distribution, generalizing it to allow for the accumulation of wealth by workers, and Pierangelo Garegnani devoted his life to promoting the (controversial) prospect of a Keynes–Sraffa synthesis. Pasinetti, who returned permanently to Italy in 1976, has since made important contributions to Post Keynesian growth theory (see Chapter 6). Outside the Sraffian tradition, Augusto Graziani and his followers developed Keynes's ideas in the *Treatise on Money* into a theory of the "monetary circuit" to explain the crisis-prone nature of capitalist economies. Although less influential than it was 30 years ago in Italy, Post Keynesian thinking continues to form a significant element in the country's economics profession (Pacella and Tortorella Esposito 2012).

The emergence of Sidney Weintraub as the first prominent Post Keynesian in the United States was due entirely to his objections to the Old Neoclassical Synthesis, which he believed to neglect wage-push inflation and to entail an ineffective and damaging deflationary response to a problem that was caused not by excessive aggregate demand but rather by the failure of wage-fixing institutions. Weintraub believed that he had discovered a magic constant: the wage share in total output. Trade union efforts to increase this share by demanding increases in money wages were therefore inevitably self-defeating, and they were also dangerously inflationary, since their only effect was to push up prices. He advocated a tax-based incomes policy to reward moderation in wage bargaining and penalize employers (and indirectly also unions) for excessive wage increases (Weintraub 1978).

Paul Davidson was first Weintraub's student and then his colleague and long-term collaborator. Davidson's *Money and the Real World* (1972) was not only an important text for the fundamentalist Keynesians but also a major event in the emergence of Post Keynesianism as a distinct school. Other landmarks were Robinson's keynote address to the 1971 meeting of the American Economic Association (Robinson 1972); the widely read 1975 survey article by Alfred Eichner and Jan Kregel published in the *Journal of Economic Literature*; and Hyman Minsky's book on *John Maynard Keynes*, which appeared in the same year (Eichner and Kregel 1975; Minsky 1975). Minsky was something of a loner, and did not get on with Davidson or publish his work in the *Journal of Post Keynesian Economics*, which Davidson and Weintraub co-edited from its inception in 1977, with financial and moral support from John Kenneth Galbraith.

Something should also be said about the two major figures in Post Keynesianism in Austria. In 1937 the young Josef Steindl had anticipated J.R. Hicks's discovery of the "supermultiplier", the Keynesian investment multiplier augmented by the accelerator effect of increased consumption, which induces a further increase in investment (Steindl 1937). After wartime exile in England, where he came under the influence of Michał Kalecki, Steindl produced his best-known book, *Maturity and Stagnation in American Capitalism* (1952), in which he argued that a growing degree of monopoly had restricted the growth of working-class consumption and thereby undermined the dynamism of capitalism in the United States. In later work Steindl explored what might be termed the post-Kaleckian issues of working-class saving, dis-saving and debt. Over a very long and highly productive career, his friend and near contemporary, Kurt Rothschild argued the case for pluralism in heterodox economics and implemented it in his own work, combining elements of Post Keynesianism, Marxism and institutionalism (Altzinger et al. 2014). Rothschild's edited volume on *Power in Economics* (1971) remains a perceptive (and unfortunately rare) attempt to grapple with some important and neglected questions concerning the treatment (and sometimes the neglect) of power relationships in the social sciences.

In the 1970s Post Keynesian ideas spread rapidly from Britain, Italy and the United States to many other parts of the world (King 2002, chapter 7). Soon there were Post Keynesians, and before long also Post Keynesian societies, in many parts of the world, including Brazil, France, Japan and the United Kingdom, and a significant presence also in Australia, Canada, Germany and Mexico. Surprisingly, there has never been a formally constituted Post Keynesian society in the United States, unlike the associations of institutionalist, radical, feminist, social and evolutionary economists that emerged during this period, and the *Journal of Post Keynesian Economics*, which commenced publication in 1977, remains the property (and under the exclusive control) of its publisher, M.E. Sharpe. There are two other English-language journals devoted to Post Keynesian ideas, both published by Edward Elgar: the *Review of Keynesian Economics*, set up in 2012, and the *European Journal of Economics and Economic Policies: Intervention*, which began life in Germany in 2004 and switched to Elgar eight years later. Post Keynesians also publish freely in heterodox journals of a more ecumenical nature, especially the *Cambridge Journal of Economics* and the *Review of Political Economy*.

Regular conferences on Post Keynesian themes in the English language are held in the United States at the University of Missouri Kansas City and at the Levy Institute of Bard College in Annandale-on-Hudson, New York (the latter devoted to Minskyan themes), and in Berlin under the auspices of the Dusseldorf-based Research Network Macroeconomics and Macroeconomic Policies (FMM), which has links to the German trade union movement. Post Keynesians also play an active role in the annual conferences of the Association for Heterodox Economics in the United Kingdom and the Society of Heterodox Economists in Australia. Details of all these activities and more can be found in the *Heterodox Economics Newsletter* that was set up in 2003 by the Post Keynesian microeconomist Fred Lee and has been edited ever since by people sympathetic to these ideas (http://heterodoxnews.com/).

References

Altzinger, W., A. Guger, P. Mooslechner and E. Nowotny (eds). 2014. *Economics as a Multi-paradigmatic Science: In Honour of Kurt W. Rothschild (1914–2010)*, Vienna: Oesterreichische Nationalbank (this is an electronic book, available at http:epub. wu.at/4305).

Arestis, P. 1992. *The Post-Keynesian Approach to Economics*, Aldershot, UK and Brookfield, VT, USA: Edward Elgar.

Arestis, P. 2009. "New Consensus macroeconomics and Keynesian critique", in E. Hein, T. Niechoj and E. Stockhammer (eds), *Macroeconomic Policies on Shaky Foundations: Whither Mainstream Economics?*, Marburg: Metropolis, pp. 165–85.

Chick, V. 1992. *On Money, Method and Keynes: Selected Essays*, Aldershot, UK and Brookfield, VT, USA: Edward Elgar.

Cornwall, W. 2012. "New Keynesian economics", in J.E. King (ed.), *The Elgar Companion to Post Keynesian Economics*, second edn, Cheltenham, UK and Northampton, MA, USA: Edward Elgar, pp. 425–9.

Davidson, P. 1972. *Money and the Real World*, London: Macmillan.

Davidson, P. 1982–83. "Rational expectations: a fallacious foundation for studying crucial decision-making processes", *Journal of Post Keynesian Economics*, 5(2), Winter, 182–96.

Davidson, P. 2011. *Post Keynesian Macroeconomic Theory, Second Edition: A Foundation for Successful Economic Policies for the Twenty-first Century*, Cheltenham, UK and Northampton, MA, USA: Edward Elgar.

Dullien, S. 2011. "The New Consensus from a traditional Keynesian and Post-Keynesian perspective: a worthwhile foundation for research, or just a waste of time?", *Economie Appliquée*, 44(1), 173–200.

Eichner, A.S. and J.A. Kregel. 1975. "An essay on Post Keynesian theory: a new paradigm in economics", *Journal of Economic Literature*, 13(4), December, 1293–314.

Forder, J. 2014. *Macroeconomics and the Phillips Curve Myth*, Oxford: Oxford University Press.

Friedman, M. 1968. "The role of monetary policy", *American Economic Review*, 58(1), March, 1–17.

Harcourt, G.C. 1972. *Some Cambridge Controversies in the Theory of Capital*, Cambridge: Cambridge University Press.

Heilbroner, R.L. and W. Milberg. 1995. *The Crisis of Vision in Modern Economic Thought*, Cambridge: Cambridge University Press.

Hicks, J.R. 1932. *The Theory of Wages*, London: Macmillan, second edition 1963.

Kaldor, N. 1956. "Alternative theories of distribution", *Review of Economic Studies*, 23(2), 83–100.

Kaldor, N. 1982. *The Scourge of Monetarism*, Oxford: Oxford University Press.

Keynes, J.M. 1936. *The General Theory of Employment, Interest and Money*, London: Macmillan.

King, J.E. 2002. *A History of Post Keynesian Economics since 1936*, Cheltenham, UK and Northampton, MA, USA: Edward Elgar.

King, J.E. 2009. *Nicholas Kaldor*, Basingstoke: Palgrave Macmillan.

Klein, L.R. 1947. *The Keynesian Revolution*, London: Macmillan.

Kuhn, T. 1962. *Structure of Scientific Revolutions*, Chicago, IL: University of Chicago Press.

Minsky, H.P. 1975. *John Maynard Keynes*, New York: Columbia University Press.

Moore, B.J. 1988. *Horizontalists and Verticalists: The Macroeconomics of Credit Money*, Cambridge: Cambridge University Press.

Pacella, A. and G. Tortorella Esposito. 2012. "Italy", in J.E. King (ed.), *The Elgar Companion to Post Keynesian Economics*, second edn, Cheltenham, UK and Northampton, MA, USA: Edward Elgar, pp. 320–24.

Palley, T.I. 2008. "After the bust: the outlook for macroeconomics and macroeconomic policy", Mimeo, Economics for Democratic and Open Societies, Washington, DC, December.

Robinson, J. 1956. *The Accumulation of Capital*, London: Macmillan.

Robinson, J. 1972. "The second crisis of economic theory", *American Economic Review*, Papers and Proceedings, **62**(2), May, 1–10.

Rogers, C. 2006. "Doing without money: a critical assessment of Woodford's analysis", *Cambridge Journal of Economics*, **30**(2), March, 293–306.

Rogers, C. 2013. "The scientific illusion of New Keynesian monetary theory", in G.C. Harcourt and P. Kriesler (eds), *The Oxford Handbook of Post-Keynesian Economics, Volume 1: Theory and Origins*, Oxford: Oxford University Press, pp. 167–87.

Rothschild, K.W. (ed.). 1971. *Power in Economics*, Harmondsworth: Penguin.

Samuelson, P.A. and R.M. Solow. 1960. "Analytical aspects of anti-inflation policy", *American Economic Review*, **50**(2), Papers and Proceedings, May, 177–94.

Sraffa, P. 1960. *Production of Commodities by Means of Commodities*, Cambridge: Cambridge University Press.

Steindl, J. 1937. "The trade cycle", trans. J.E. King, *Review of Political Economy* (2008), **20**(3), July, 341–8.

Steindl, J. 1952. *Maturity and Stagnation in American Capitalism*, Oxford: Blackwell, second edition 1976, New York: Monthly Review Press.

Stiglitz, J.E. 2010. *Free Fall: America, Free Markets, and the Sinking of the World Economy*, revised edn, New York: Norton.

Vercelli, A. 1991. *Methodological Foundations of Macroeconomics: Keynes and Lucas*, Cambridge: Cambridge University Press.

Weintraub, S. 1978. *Capitalism's Inflation and Unemployment Crisis: Beyond Monetarism and Keynesianism*, Reading, MA: Addison-Wesley.

Woodford, M. 2003. *Interest and Prices: Foundations of a Theory of Monetary Policy*, Princeton, NJ: Princeton University Press.

4 Some methodological issues

Why bother with methodology?

Like the fictional character who was astonished to discover that he had been talking in prose all his life, many economists would be surprised to find that they practise methodology in their everyday research and teaching. And yet they do. The theories that they write about and expound to students, the techniques that they use to assess the evidence that may (or may not) be relevant to these theories – all this presupposes a methodological position (or a variety of positions) on the nature of the economic universe (ontology) and how best to learn about it (epistemology). This raises important questions concerning the validity of a pluralist approach to economic theory, the role of formalism (the use of mathematical models and econometric techniques) and the supposed need to provide "microfoundations" for macroeconomics. Economists should at least be aware of what these methodological issues are, and of the strengths and potential weaknesses of the solutions that are proposed for them.

As with several other heterodox schools, Post Keynesians have always taken a strong interest in questions of methodology – too much interest, according to some, who believe that excessive concern with the philosophy of science has distracted their attention from more pressing matters of economic theory and public policy (Fontana and Gerrard 2006). The story begins with Keynes, whose doctoral dissertation was substantially complete by 1914 but only published, as *A Treatise on Probability*, seven years later (Keynes 1921 [1973]). Largely ignored for almost half a century, the *Treatise* was rediscovered by Post Keynesians in the 1980s, and a substantial critical literature soon developed (Carabelli 1988; O'Donnell 1989). The questions that Keynes had raised were, to repeat, issues of methodology: how to theorize, how to conduct empirical research and how to formulate sensible public policy, in a world in which fundamental uncertainty made the assignment of numerical probabilities to future outcomes distinctly problematic. Possibly too much attention was indeed paid to these matters in the 1990s, but we neglect them at our peril.

If you remain unconvinced, consider this example. James Crotty lists the 13 assumptions required by the theory of efficient (financial) markets, which include homogeneous expectations ("there is no disagreement about future cash flows among agents") (No. 4); rational expectations ("the statistical distributions of future cash flows are known with certainty") (No. 6); and – astonishingly – "No one can default" (No. 12). As he comments, this set of assumptions is not an approximation to reality, but rather a severe distortion of reality (Crotty 2013, p. 145). Its protagonists justify the unrealism of their assumptions by reference to Milton Friedman's influential "methodology of positive economics", according to which it is only the predictions generated by a theory that are relevant; the assumptions that it relies on simply do not matter (Friedman 1953). This position is probably better characterized as "instrumentalism" – the claim that theories are nothing but useful instruments for generating predictions – than as "positivism", a notoriously slippery term that seems to be given a different meaning each time it is used.

It is, to say the very least, a highly contentious position. "The proposition that crudely unrealistic assumptions are not inferior to realistic assumptions in theory construction must be distinguished", as Crotty observes, "from the more reasonable proposition that some degree of abstraction – or approximation of reality – is necessary in theory building" (Crotty 2013, p. 139). It can have profoundly important consequences in the real world. In the United States it was these "crudely unrealistic assumptions" that led the regulators who were inspired by efficient market theory to allow banks to become dangerously risky and to adopt a cavalier attitude to debt, to incur excessive leverage and to ignore the possibility that their debtors might default. The irrelevance of more sensible assumptions, which might have avoided these regulatory failures and prevented the financial crisis of 2007–08, was justified on methodological grounds. Methodology matters!

There are two excellent books on Post Keynesian methodology (Dow 1996; Jespersen 2009), and another very good critical introduction to the use of analogies and models in economics more generally (Birks 2014). In this chapter I can only touch on a few of the many important issues that they raise. I begin by discussing questions of ontology, and then proceed to the arguments for (and against) pluralism in economics, as interpreted by Post Keynesians. Next I deal with controversies concerning the use of formal modelling in economics, before turning to the vexed question of microfoundations.

Questions of ontology

First and foremost, something must be said about the nature of the economic universe. Keynes was convinced that it differed significantly from the natural world, and (in an often-quoted passage in his obituary for Marshall, reprinted in his *Essays in Biography*), invoked the authority of the great German physicist Max Planck, who had "once remarked to me that in early life he had thought of studying economics, but had found it too difficult!" (Keynes 1951, p. 158n). Of course, Keynes continued, he did not mean that mathematical economics was beyond him.

> But the amalgam of logic and intuition, and the wide knowledge of facts, most of which are not precise, which is required for economic interpretation in its highest form is, quite truly, overwhelming for those whose gift mainly consists in the power to imagine and pursue to their furthest points the implications and prior conditions of comparatively simple facts which are known with a high degree of precision. (p. 158n)

Keynes criticized Edgeworth's approach to the subject for similar reasons:

> The atomic hypothesis which has worked so splendidly in Physics breaks down in Psychics. We are faced at every turn with the problems of Organic Unity, of Discreteness, of Discontinuity – the whole is not equal to the sum of the parts, comparisons of quantity fail us, small changes produce large effects, the assumptions of a uniform and homogeneous continuum are not satisfied. (Keynes 1951, pp. 232–3)

These observations, ignored by the great majority of New Keynesians and denied in their everyday theoretical and empirical practice, are taken very seriously by Post Keynesians.

As we saw in Chapter 2, Paul Davidson identifies non-ergodicity as one of the three crucial axioms of mainstream economic theory that Keynes denied. We cannot be sure that the future will be like the past. Economic events are not precisely predictable, like the precise times of high and low tides and the exact dates and times of solar and lunar eclipses. Short of major cosmic disasters (meteor impacts, for example), predictions of future eclipses can be made today for centuries ahead, and we can be confident that they will not be falsified. But the economic future is not like that. It is impossible to make accurate predictions of unemployment levels, exchange rates, wage levels or gross domestic product (GDP) growth a few months ahead, let alone millennia. This is what gives rise to fundamental (Keynesian) uncertainty, and makes the "physics envy" of orthodox economists quite pointless, as Max Planck recognized.

But Davidson's interpretation is itself problematic (O'Donnell 2014–15). It rests on what Sheila Dow has identified as "dualistic" thinking, which imposes "either/or", "A or not-A", mutually exclusive categories of thought on a reality that is generally much more complicated than this, and needs to be conceived of in terms of a continuum rather than a dichotomy. The principle of the excluded middle is a feature of Cartesian–Euclidian thought, which Dow rejects in favour of the more subtle and open-ended Babylonian mode of thinking (Dow 1996, chapter 2). Note that this distinction is not itself a dual, since Babylonian logic is necessarily pluralistic. All varieties of mainstream macroeconomics, from Old Keynesian theory to the New Neoclassical Synthesis, are Cartesian–Euclidian in their underlying methodology, not Babylonian.

This is related to the important distinction between closed-system and open-system thinking:

> An open system is one where not all the constituent variables and structural relationships are known or knowable, and thus the boundaries of the system are not known or knowable. This is the province of fuzzy mathematics, with indeterminate boundaries of sets . . . It is also the province of non-classical logic, where logical relations are applied to uncertain knowledge; this logic is variously known as ordinary logic or human logic. (Dow 1996, p. 14)

This is the logic of Keynes's *Treatise on Probability*. If reality is understood in the Babylonian manner as an open system, Dow concludes, there is scope for free will, creativity and the evolution of individuals and institutions in ways that may be difficult to predict with any degree of precision.

It suggests that atomistic, reductionist ways of thinking are likely to be less productive than a more organic approach: "An organic system involves interdependencies which preclude the selection of one set of axioms as universally causal; it also involves interdependencies which are complex and evolutionary, and thus not amenable to formalization with respect to separable elements within a single system of reasoning" (Dow 1996, p. 15). Dow concedes that partial closure may be possible, so that the use of formal mathematical and statistical methods is not entirely excluded, but cautions that such partial closures are "always open organically to influences from other parts of the overall system" (p. 14).

I shall return to these issues in Chapter 9 in the context of the relationship between Post Keynesianism and evolutionary political economy, where the open-ended and unpredictable nature of evolutionary processes and their affinity with open systems thinking will be seen to be highly relevant. Some Post Keynesians would go further than this, and advocate "critical realism" as the appropriate methodological stance (Fullbrook 2009). Its most prominent advocate is Tony Lawson (1997, 2003). Lawson draws on the work of the philosopher Roy Bhaskar, who pointed to the stratification of social reality, with each layer being causally irreducible to those below it. Deep social structures and underlying causal mechanisms are not directly observable, Bhaskar maintained, but can be inferred from observed reality through a process of "retroduction". For Lawson, these underlying structures and mechanisms are much more important and more interesting than the superficial event regularities identified by mainstream economists. These fundamental tenets of critical realism have always guided the work of many Post Keynesians, whether or not they have been conscious of it. Even Kalecki, it can be argued, was a critical realist in practice, even though he published almost nothing on questions of methodology and died before the appearance of Bhaskar's principal works (Jefferson and King 2011).

There has been "a general, though cautious, acceptance of critical realism by leading Post Keynesians" (Brown 2012, p. 124), no doubt aided by the fact that it is very much a Cambridge phenomenon, with Lawson running a Critical Realist Workshop there for many years and maintaining close relations with the (relatively few) remaining Post Keynesians there. But reservations have been expressed about Lawson's dismissal of all event regularities in economics, and there is some disagreement about the precise implications for econometric research and the use of formal methods more generally, as will be seen later in this chapter. Lawson's own latest thoughts on all these questions can be found in his recent extended critical account of neoclassical economics (Lawson 2013).

Pluralism and the Post Keynesians

Dow correctly identifies the Babylonian method as a powerful argument for pluralism in economics. In fact there are (at least) five arguments for pluralism, two of them convincingly advocated by Kurt Rothschild (2006). The first argument draws on the complexity of the social and economic world, and the impossibility of understanding it all by means of a single theoretical or analytical apparatus; this is part of the motivation for Dow's advocacy of the Babylonian method. The second argument concerns the need for economic (and social) theory to be socially and historically specific, so that it is different for different stages of (capitalist) history and changes as capitalism itself changes. This argument is derived from Marx, but commands much broader acceptance, notably from institutionalist and evolutionary economists as well as from Post Keynesians. It is especially pertinent to the Post Keynesian way of thinking about economic growth and development, as will be seen in Chapter 6.

There are three additional arguments for pluralism in economics that Rothschild did not place much weight on (but would probably not have dissented from). With allowance for American spelling, they can be summarized as the "three e's": evolutionary, ethical and esthetic. The evolutionary argument is well presented by Hodgson and Rothman (1999) in their critique of the biased publication decisions of the editors of leading economics journals. Evolution proceeds by means of natural selection; this requires diversity, or there is nothing to select from. Evolution is a necessary condition for progress (though not a sufficient condition), and the lack of diversity is therefore a sufficient condition for lack of progress. Less extremely put, progress will be delayed, if not prevented altogether, if a monolithic mainstream attempts to suppress all forms of heterodoxy and dissent.

The ethical argument is very simple: economists are supposed to believe in the benefits of competition, and yet they are strangely reluctant to accept it in matters pertaining to their own discipline. This, of course, is connected to the political implications of economic theories, which will be discussed in Chapter 7. The esthetic argument is equally simple, if (perhaps) a little self-indulgent: diverse landscapes are more beautiful than monotonous ones (compare Cumbria with Essex, or Montana with Kansas). Conferences of heterodox economists are much more interesting – here I speak from long experience – than conferences dominated by mainstream economists. Economics does not have to be boring!

There is, of course, a case against pluralism, which has to do with the need to preserve some minimal degree of coherence, and thus to rule out confused, unintelligible and internally inconsistent arguments, theories and models. This necessarily imposes some limits to pluralism, though it is vital that it be done cautiously: what is unintelligible to one person may simply appear to be badly written to another. It is not immediately obvious what criteria might help us to distinguish between improvable and unimprovable texts (Dow 2014).

Formalism: mathematics and econometrics

These abstruse controversies in the philosophy of science do have implications for the practice of economics, since they bear directly on the case for and against the use of formal modelling in theory construction and on the employment of econometric techniques in empirical research. At one extreme, many Post Keynesians take the value of formalism for granted and use whatever mathematical and statistical tools are available to them; Hein (2012) is a good example. At the other extreme, Lawson argues that formalism is almost always inappropriate to the open systems that characterize economic reality, and is best avoided in almost all circumstances. It invariably involves the introduction of "highly artificial" and "bogus abstractions", which are "designed to achieve mathematical tractability, system closure and completeness . . . rather than an understanding of the real causal mechanisms at work" (Lawson 1997, p. 233).

It should be remembered that the compulsory use of formal techniques is a relatively recent phenomenon in mainstream economics. The extent of the transformation of the discipline that has taken place over the last 70 years or so should not be underestimated. The September 1944 issue of the *American Economic Review*, for example, contained six main articles, none of them on neoclassical economic theory and all without a single equation or diagram. The only theoretical piece in the entire issue was a brief note on the incidence of profit taxation by the future institutionalist Kenneth Boulding, which did include two elaborate diagrams but (again) no equations. The contrast with today's *American Economic Review* could not be greater (King 2015, p. 119).

In fact some Post Keynesians have made widespread use of econometric methods since the 1980s, when Alfred Eichner estimated structural equations for a short-period macroeconometric model of the US economy and Philip Arestis carried out similar work in the United Kingdom (Downward 2012, p. 132). Casual inspection of recent issues of the principal Post Keynesian journals will confirm that a significant proportion (perhaps the majority) of published papers continue to use either cross-sectional or time-series econometrics in addition to descriptive statistics and other types of informal empirical evidence. This is perhaps in part a pragmatic question of career advancement (or sheer survival), with Post Keynesians using econometrics as a form of rhetoric to demonstrate that they are technically as competent as mainstream economists.

But there is more to it than this. If "the assumptions involved in estimating coefficients are shared with all (even descriptive) empirical analysis ... then logically any empirical analysis advocated by Post Keynesians can embrace econometric *estimation*" (Downward 2012, p. 136, emphasis in the original). Indeed, the overriding Post Keynesian concern with economic policy issues might suggest that they *must* embrace econometric estimation of the signs and approximate magnitudes of such critical variables as fiscal policy multipliers. How else would they be able to predict the consequences (for example) of the austerity measures that are inflicting so much damage on the eurozone?

Even Lawson concedes the existence of "demi-regs", which are partial and temporary regularities that offer the potential for partial and provisional closure, implying that formal methods may be applicable for some problems, under some conditions, when used carefully and with discretion. Most Post Keynesians would agree that some degree of formalism is indeed essential for a proper understanding of the business cycle, of the process of economic growth and of the relationship between cycles and growth. Michał Kalecki's pioneering work on these questions in the mid 1930s almost certainly placed him in the top 1 per cent of mathematical economists of the time (Kalecki 1935). At the same time, as will be seen in Chapter 6, mathematical modelling is by no means the whole story, with Post Keynesian growth theorists recognizing the need also for much more informal reasoning that draws upon history, politics and institutional change.

A suitably nuanced conclusion to these controversies was provided by Victoria Chick in a paper entitled "On the importance of knowing one's place", in which she argues that formal methods should indeed be used in economics, but they should be confined to appropriate areas. "Formal techniques are powerful tools, but they can also be dangerous; the problem is to identify applications where they can be used safely" (Chick 1998, p. 1859). Axiomatization, precision and atomism all have advantages, but they also carry the risk that economic theorists are led to neglect the irreducibly limited and imperfect nature of human knowledge. Thus technical advances in economics are not neutral. Their application to the *General Theory*, to take one important example, led to radical changes in the way in which Keynes's analysis was understood (p. 1865), as I suggested in Chapter 3. "Formalism is fine", Chick concludes, "but it must know its place. Economists need to debate further the boundaries of that place" (p. 1868).

What, precisely, is ruled out by these considerations? There is no simple or universally applicable answer. Just as "some degree of abstraction" is unavoidable in any attempt to theorize about the economy, so "some degree of formalism" is also necessary and helpful. Precisely how much formalism is justified in any particular case remains, always and inevitably, a matter of judgement. As already noted, these difficult issues continue to divide Post Keynesians. This, however, is a better situation than exists in mainstream economics, where there is very little discussion, and almost no questioning, of the limits to formal modelling.

The microfoundations delusion

As I have argued elsewhere at considerable length (King 2012), the microfoundations metaphor has been used by mainstream economists to support a micro-reduction strategy, whereby macroeconomics is reduced to microeconomics. More precisely, the intention is to reduce macroeconomic theory to statements about individuals: RARE individuals (representative agents with rational expectations), maximizing lifetime utility subject to random shocks in a Dynamic Stochastic General Equilibrium (DSGE) framework. This project is (fortunately) doomed to failure, but this (unfortunately) has not prevented a minority of Post Keynesians – who are most definitely not in favour of micro-reduction – from using the metaphor of microfoundations and thereby appearing to endorse the project.

The consequences are extremely serious. At a conference on the New Neoclassical Synthesis in December 2005, Simon Wren-Lewis, an economic adviser to the British government, contrasted two "methodological approaches":

> The pre-microfoundations approach puts the stress on data consistency: models that are not consistent with the data (in an econometric sense) should be rejected. In contrast, the Bank of England's new model embodies a quite different approach. Internal consistency is vital, because only then can we be sure that relationships are consistent with the axioms of microeconomic theory. Econometric consistency is not essential (it is "handled" via ad hoc, non-core relationships), but instead is a pointer to future theoretical development. (Wren-Lewis 2007, pp. 47–8)

Thus micro-reduction, and the associated microfoundations metaphor, is an integral part of the retreat from realism on the part of mainstream macroeconomists.

There are at least two reasons why micro-reduction will not succeed in economics: the fallacy of composition and downward causation. They are separate, and each is sufficient to condemn micro-reduction to failure (so that neither is necessary). Note that the objection is to explanatory or epistemological reduction. No one objects to the trivial and uninteresting principle of ontological reduction, which tells us that society is made up (or composed) of individuals, just as individuals are made up of their body parts. But society cannot be completely explained in terms of the properties of these individuals, just as you and I are more than the sum of our body parts.

Evolutionary economists sometime adduce a third reason for the failure of micro-reduction. This is the prevalence of emergent properties of economic and social systems, properties that cannot be inferred even from complete knowledge of the individuals that make up the system. Emergent properties seem to be a very frequent consequence of complexity in economic and social life, while fallacies of composition and downward causation can be found even in very simple systems. For reasons of space I shall ignore this very interesting third argument against micro-reduction and concentrate on the first two.

There are a number of well-established examples of the fallacy of composition in economics (Lavoie 2014, pp. 16–22 provides an extended discussion). Probably the best known is the "paradox of thrift", which was emphasized by Keynes: any individual agent can increase her saving, should she choose to do so, but if all agents attempt to do so, without any increase in aggregate investment, the result will be a decline in output and income, leaving aggregate saving unchanged. Interestingly enough, the 1930s version of this argument originated not with Keynes but with the future Nobel laureate, Ragnar Frisch. In a 1932 radio broadcast in Norway (four years before the publication of the *General Theory*), Frisch maintained that it was necessary to encourage consumer spending in order to stimulate output and employment. If instead society tried to save more, the result would be a fall in income and a reduction in saving. Frisch's argument was recently recalled, approvingly, by another Nobel Prize winner, Lawrence Klein (2006, p. 171).

There is also a Kaleckian "paradox of costs": wage increases are invariably bad news for any individual capitalist enterprise, since they push up costs and reduce profits, but under certain circumstances they may be good news for capitalists as a whole, since they increase effective demand and thus raise output and aggregate profits. The distinction between "wage-led" and "profit-led regimes", which is discussed in Chapters 7 and 8, is an important implication of the paradox of costs.

A "paradox of liquidity" is also implicit in both Keynes and Minsky: any individual enterprise that wishes to become more liquid can normally do so, at a price, but if all enterprises attempt to increase their liquidity the effect will merely be to push up interest rates, and in some circumstances to cause a major financial crisis. Finally, it should be remembered that there is an international dimension to the problem, so that a potential fallacy of composition can easily be committed in the analysis of a nation's economic relations with the rest of the world. Any one state can become more competitive than the rest, for example, by depreciating its currency or by forcing down real wages and unit labour costs, but this is not possible for Planet Earth as a whole.

Downward causation refers to the fact (again, a rather obvious one) that individuals are deeply influenced by the society in which they live, and the economy that is embedded in it. Our tastes and preferences, our values and beliefs, our knowledge and skills, all depend heavily on social forces, and when those forces change, we change with them. The consequences become apparent when we consider the meaning of "microfoundations". It is a constructional metaphor, and its use is impossible to reconcile with downward causation. When a house is being built, the foundations are put in place first and they do not change, either when the house itself is constructed upon them or, later, when the house is redecorated, refurbished, renovated and (within quite broad limits) reconstructed. In constructing a house, there *is* no downward causation. Thus the metaphor is inapplicable to human society, where downward causation is so pervasive and so influential.

Some Post Keynesians, recognizing this problem, have suggested that we need to supply "macrofoundations" for microeconomics. But this conjures up a strange image – a house with the foundations on top of the roof! It is surely better to avoid constructional metaphors altogether, or at least to replace vertical analogies with horizontal ones. As Kalecki maintained, macroeconomics and microeconomics should be thought of as existing side by side, closely related to and influencing each other but also relatively autonomous and neither constituting the foundations of the other (Kriesler 1996). Certainly Post Keynesians do need their own microeconomic theory, which must be different from that of the mainstream and consistent with Post Keynesian macroeconomics. This is the subject of the following chapter.

References

Birks, S. 2014. *Rethinking Economics: From Analogies to the Real World*, Dordrecht: Springer.

Brown, A. 2012. "Critical realism", in J.E. King (ed.), *The Elgar Companion to Post Keynesian Economics*, second edn, Cheltenham, UK and Northampton, MA, USA: Edward Elgar, pp. 121–6.

Carabelli, A.M. 1988. *On Keynes's Method*, London: Macmillan.

Chick, V. 1998. "On the importance of knowing one's place: the role of formalism in economics", *Economic Journal*, **108**(451), November, 1859–69.

Crotty, J. 2013. "The realism of assumptions does matter: why Keynes-Minsky theory must replace efficient market theory as the guide to financial regulation policy", in M.H. Wolfson and G.A. Epstein (eds), *The Handbook of the Political Economy of Financial Crises*, Oxford: Oxford University Press, pp. 133–58.

Dow, S.C. 1996. *The Methodology of Macroeconomic Thought*, Cheltenham, UK and Brookfield, VT, USA: Edward Elgar.

Dow, S.C. 2014. "Consistency in pluralism and microfoundations", Mimeo, University of Stirling.

Downward, P. 2012. "Econometrics", in J.E. King (ed.), *The Elgar Companion to Post Keynesian Economics*, second edn, Cheltenham, UK and Northampton, MA, USA: Edward Elgar, pp. 132–8.

Fontana, G. and B. Gerarrd. 2006. "The future of Post Keynesian economics", *Banca Nazionale del Lavoro Quarterly Review*, **59**(236), 49–80.

Friedman, M. 1953. "The methodology of positive economics", in M. Friedman, *Essays in Positive Economics*, Chicago, IL: Chicago University Press, pp. 3–43.

Fullbrook, E. (ed.). 2009. *Ontology and Economics: Tony Lawson and his Critics*, London and New York: Routledge.

Hein, E. 2012. *The Macroeconomics of Finance-dominated Capitalism – and Its Crisis*, Cheltenham, UK and Northampton, MA, USA: Edward Elgar.

Hodgson, G.M. and H. Rothman. 1999. "The editors and authors of economics journals: a case of institutional oligopoly", *Economic Journal*, **109**(453), February, F165–F186.

Jefferson, T. and J.E. King. 2011. "Michał Kalecki and critical realism", *Cambridge Journal of Economics*, **35**(5), September, 957–72.

Jespersen, J. 2009. *Macroeconomic Methodology: A Post Keynesian Perspective*, Cheltenham, UK and Northampton, MA, USA: Edward Elgar.

Kalecki, M. 1935. "A macro-dynamic theory of business cycles", *Econometrica*, **3**(3), July, 327–44, reprinted in J. Osiatýnski (ed.), *Collected Works of Michał Kalecki. Volume 1. Capitalism, Business Cycles and Full Employment*, Oxford: Clarendon Press, 1990, pp. 120–38.

Keynes, J.M. 1921. *A Treatise on Probability*, London: Macmillan; reprinted in *The Collected Writings of John Maynard Keynes* (1973), Vol. VIII, London: Macmillan, 1973.

Keynes, J.M. 1951. *Essays in Biography*, second edn, London: Rupert Hart-Davis.

King, J.E. 2012. *The Microfoundations Delusion: Metaphor and Dogma in the History of Macroeconomics*, Cheltenham, UK and Northampton, MA, USA: Edward Elgar.

King, J.E. 2015. "United States of America", in V. Barnett (ed.), *Routledge Handbook of the History of Global Economic Thought*, London and New York: Routledge, pp. 113–29.

Klein, L.R. 2006. "Paul Samuelson as a 'Keynesian' economist", in M. Szenberg, L. Ramrattan and A.A. Gottesman (eds), *Samuelsonian Economics and the Twenty-first Century*, Oxford: Oxford University Press, pp. 165–77.

Kriesler, P. 1996. "Microfoundations: a Kaleckian perspective", in J.E. King (ed.), *An Alternative Macroeconomic Theory: The Kaleckian Model and Post-Keynesian Economics*, Boston, MA, Dordrecht and London: Kluwer, pp. 55–72.

Lavoie, M. 2014. *Post-Keynesian Economics: New Foundations*, Cheltenham, UK and Northampton, MA, USA: Edward Elgar.

Lawson, T. 1997. *Economics and Reality*, London and New York: Routledge.

Lawson, T. 2003. *Reorienting Economics*, London and New York: Routledge.

Lawson, T. 2013. "What is the 'school' called neoclassical economics?", *Cambridge Journal of Economics*, **37**(5), September, 947–83.

O'Donnell, R.M. 1989. *Keynes: Philosophy, Economics and Politics. The Philosophical Foundations of Keynes's Thought and their Influence on his Economics and Politics*, London: Macmillan.

O'Donnell, R.M. 2014–15. "A critique of the ergodic/non-ergodic approach to uncertainty", *Journal of Post Keynesian Economics*, **37**(2), Winter, 187–209.

Rothschild, K.W. 2006. "Economics past and present. An interview with Kurt W. Rothchild", *EAEPE Newsletter*, **36**, July–August, 11–14.

Wren-Lewis, S. 2007. "Are there dangers in the microfoundations consensus?", in P. Arestis (ed.), *Is There a New Consensus in Macroeconomics?*, Basingstoke: Palgrave Macmillan, pp. 43–60.

5   Post Keynesian microeconomics

A methodological prelude

First, some general points by way of introduction. Post Keynesian microeconomics draws heavily from the work of other heterodox or quasi-heterodox schools, especially institutionalism but also behavioural economics and evolutionary political economy, and perhaps has the potential to contribute original ideas of its own to these schools. I shall have more to say on this question in Chapter 9. Moreover, the methodological differences between Post Keynesian and mainstream microeconomics are substantial. Above all, realism (or at least "realisticness") is regarded as much more important than mathematical tractability.

Here three points in particular must be stressed. First, we are dealing with a capitalist economy, in which it is firms, not individual consumers (or households), that make the running. This is why this chapter starts with the firm, and its pricing and investment decisions, and not with consumers and their utility functions. It is corporate profits that drive the economy, not consumer preferences. Second, markets are imperfect: the majority of firms enjoy some degree of product market power, and they are price makers, not price takers; there is no Walrasian auctioneer. Moreover, most markets are oligopolistic: we are dealing with "competition among the few", not with textbook monopoly or with large group imperfect competition.

Third, and most important, the pervasive influence of fundamental uncertainty means that precise maximization strategies are difficult or impossible to implement. Joan Robinson came to regard the neglect of this factor as one of the most significant defects of her highly influential *Economics of Imperfect Competition* (Robinson 1969). Expectations are crucial, and they cannot be reduced to certainty-equivalents. We have already encountered this problem in the context of Keynes's reference to "animal spirits" as an important element in the firm's investment decisions. Future costs may not be easy to predict, and future revenues are even more uncertain. There is a link between the Post Keynesian theory of the firm and behavioural economists like Herbert Simon, who also emphasize the prevalence of "satisficing" rather than maximizing behaviour, and focus on the use of conventions and rules of thumb.

At all events, Post Keynesians have always shied away from general equilibrium models, in their microeconomics as well as in their macro-economic theory. They have generally also been unimpressed by most versions of game theory, since they believe both the objective functions and the pay-offs to be subject to fundamental uncertainty that is not reducible, via probability estimates, to certainty-equivalence. This does not rule out all formal modelling, but it does constrain it to take account of these complexities of the real capitalist world.

The Post Keynesian firm

The Post Keynesian firm is a corporation, not an owner-managed individual enterprise. The influence of the work of Berle and Means (1932) on the separation of ownership and control has been considerable, and (though he is rarely cited in the literature) James Burnham's notion of the "managerial revolution" has also permeated the analysis. Once again, Post Keynesians have drawn heavily on institutionalist thinking, and John Kenneth Galbraith's conception of the *New Industrial State*, controlled not by traditional capitalist owners but by the managerial "technostructure", has also been influential (Galbraith 1967). The substantial modifications to this view of the firm that seem to be required in the new stage of financialization and neoliberal capitalism will be considered in Chapter 8.

Hence Post Keynesian pricing and investment theory places considerable emphasis on the role of market power, which is seen as being combined with (and partly caused by) technological economies of scale and scope. It follows that in almost all Post Keynesian microeconomic models output is constrained by demand, not by rising costs. Direct costs tend to be constant over a wide range of output, which permits an input–output framework to be used in dealing with production, with roughly constant input coefficients and relatively little scope for substitution between inputs (especially capital and labour) in response to changes in their relative prices.

A good summary of the relevant evidence on pricing behaviour is provided by Coutts and Norman (2013, p. 460). Increases in demand tend to be met by some combination of increased output and lengthening order books. Higher costs are more likely than greater demand to induce price increases, but there is an asymmetry here, since reduced demand often does lead to price reductions. Mark-up pricing is common even in highly competitive markets, but it is even more common under oligopoly. And the prevalence of mark-up pricing is high, both in manufacturing and in service industries.

Two final common elements in Post Keynesian price theory are the existence of barriers to entry and the role of finance. Entry barriers are seen as necessary to maintain the firm's market power, and entry-prevention strategies are seen as a major factor in the firm's pricing decisions, with scale economies and (increasingly) intellectual property regarded as the main sources of these barriers. As for finance, Post Keynesians reject both the efficient markets hypothesis and the Modigliani–Miller theorem, so that the level of corporate debt *does* matter. Early work on this question came from Kalecki (1937), who regarded both "borrowers' risk" and "lenders' risk" as reasons why oligopolies do not generally become monopolies. Beyond a certain point, he argued, managers are reluctant to borrow and lenders are unwilling to increase their financial commitments to any individual enterprise. This points to a major role for internal finance (retained profits) in pricing decisions, to credit rationing as a potentially serious constraint on the expansion of the firm and in particular to the cyclical variability of finance, as insisted by Minsky, as a factor in investment decisions (and in their instability over the business cycle).

These are the common elements in what is actually a wide variety of Post Keynesian pricing models. The earliest was again that of Kalecki, who linked it to the question of income distribution. His oligopolists apply a mark-up to the average variable costs of production, which he takes to consist of the wages of shop-floor labour and the raw materials bill, but not the salaries of the office staff. The size of the mark-up depends on the degree of monopoly in the product market. Aggregating over the entire manufacturing sector, Kalecki's formula for the distribution of income between labour and capital shows that the share of profits in GDP is a positive function of the average degree of monopoly and of the price of raw materials, relative to industrial goods. In the final version of his model, Kalecki (1971) also allowed for the bargaining power of organized labour, which was able, he now believed, to constrain profit mark-ups and thus to increase the share of wages at the expense of profits.

Other approaches to the pricing problem have also proved influential. In the pricing models of Philip Andrews (1949) and Paolo Sylos-Labini (1961), the critical factor in the determination of the mark-up is the desire to prevent the entry of new competitors into the market; pricing decisions are essentially forward-looking. In the Cambridge pricing models of Adrian Wood (1975) and Geoff Harcourt and Peter Kenyon (1976), the crucial factor is the firm's need for internal finance. The watchword is now "retain and reinvest", with profit seen as the road to growth (and hence also as the road to security, since it is assumed that large and rapidly growing firms are less likely to be taken over or driven into bankruptcy).

Ironically, this view of the firm's pricing decisions seemed to be even more directly relevant to late socialist Hungary than to the capitalist West. Managers in the quasi-market system of the 1980s had an insatiable desire for investment, and set their prices accordingly. "The more the profit motive fades, the higher the profit level tends to be, since in a decentralised socialist economy investment decisions are made by managers interested only in the growth of the enterprise" (Szego 1991, p. 336, original emphasis removed). Even in the capitalist West, similar motivations could be ascribed to corporate managers, as in effect they were by Alfred Eichner (1975, 1987), who provided the first comprehensive Post Keynesian model of pricing and investment. A synthetic model is provided by Marc Lavoie (2014, chapter 3), with the firm's rate of growth and profit rate determined by the intersection of the "finance frontier" (given by the availability of retained earnings) and the "expansion frontier" (that shows a U-shaped relationship between the firm's profit rate and the rate at which it expands output).

This is broad-brush material. A very much more nuanced approach was taken by Fred Lee (1998, 2013), who drew on literature from organization theory and management accounting to distinguish a number of similar but interestingly different rules for setting the mark-up that were applied by large corporations. Lee remained dissatisfied with the outcome. "My position is that we really do not know how the profit mark up is really determined because no one has done the hard work of going into enterprises to find out" (personal communication, 22 April 2014). Sadly Lee died in late 2014, before he had been able to complete the necessary hard work (Jo and Todorova 2015).

Although most – as we saw in Chapter 4, not all – Post Keynesians eschew the microfoundations metaphor, they all recognize the substantial macroeconomic implications of the theory of the firm for the determinants of relative income shares, aggregate investment, effective demand, employment and (in the long run) the rate of economic growth. Thus Josef Steindl extended his thinking on the life cycles of firms and products to encompass the maturity and stagnation of US capitalism as a system; and he later had second thoughts (King 1995b). His early work influenced the "monopoly capital" school of American Marxism, led by Paul Baran and Paul Sweezy, and fits rather well with more recent Post Keynesian models of the different stages of global capitalist development, which we shall encounter in subsequent chapters in the context of growth theory (Chapter 6) and the origins of the Global Financial Crisis (Chapter 8).

There are also, inevitably, some unresolved issues. In the digital economy, while it is not always clear exactly what is being produced (disks and instruction booklets? knowledge? entertainment?), it does often seem to be the case that fixed costs are very large while average variable cost is very low. Full-cost pricing might work under such conditions, but other variants of mark-up pricing will not. This is connected to the greatly increased value of intangible assets, above all intellectual property, and the very powerful, but also temporary, barriers to entry that can be erected through patents, trademarks and copyright law. Joseph Schumpeter would have recognized the new digital firm; Kalecki and Steindl might have been puzzled by it. Finally, a whole set of questions is posed by the emergence of a new stage of financialized capital, which seems to be rendering the "stakeholder theory of the firm" obsolete and undermining the autonomy of management. This question will be discussed in Chapter 8, but it does have implications for the firm's treatment of its labour, to which we now turn.

The labour market

The fallacy of composition is more dangerous in the analysis of labour markets than in any other aspect of microeconomic theory. The *ceteris paribus* clause is clearly inapplicable here, since earnings from employment still constitute more than half of all income and are the most important single determinant of consumption expenditure. Cutting wages will reduce consumer spending, thereby shifting product and labour demand curves inwards. Moreover, as we saw in Chapter 2, the "labour market" is not a true market in the Walrasian sense, since variations in the price of labour (the real wage) cannot be relied upon to clear the market. Thus the level of employment and the unemployment rate depend on factors outside the labour market: specifically, on the level of effective demand. They are determined in the product market.

There is one other significant implication of the Post Keynesian rejection of microfoundations as applied to the labour market. Downward causation is especially important here, since the characteristics of labour markets in conditions of full employment are profoundly different from those that prevail when there is substantial involuntary unemployment. Only under full employment is it possible for a worker to be indifferent to the loss of her job, since only then is it possible for her to find an equally good job right away. Only then is it possible for the labour supply curve to the firm to be perfectly elastic. Only under full employment, then, is it possible for labour markets to be perfectly competitive. Whenever there is significant involuntary unemployment, labour markets are not perfectly competitive: workers have good reason to value their jobs, since they can expect some difficulty in finding equally suitable employment, and so they will not leave in response to the slightest reduction in wages. Unless there is full employment, therefore, the labour supply curve to the firm is upward-sloping, employers enjoy some degree of monopsony power and a simple negative relationship between the real wage and the level of employment can no longer be relied upon, even at the microeconomic level, in individual labour markets.

This is actually a rather straightforward implication of the neoclassical theory of the firm, though it is not taken into account by mainstream labour economists as often as it should be. But there are good reasons for dissatisfaction with neoclassical labour economics, conceived more broadly. Bounded rationality applies in the workplace, perhaps more so than in other aspects of economic life. "People look for a better job only when they are seriously dissatisfied with the one that they have; likewise, employers do not appraise, rank, dismiss and reappoint their entire labour force at the beginning of each working day" (King 2001, p.66). And the workplace is not just a site of income generation. It is also a social institution, in which "considerations of emulation and envy on the one hand and of fairness and solidarity on the other hand help explain why individuals join unions, develop commitments to informal work groups, and worry more (as Keynes believed) about relative wages than about the trade-off between leisure and consumer goods" (p. 66). In all this there are affinities between Post Keynesian labour economics and institutionalist and Marxian thinking on the employment relationship. Institutionalists have always stressed that labour markets are deeply embedded in social relations. Like Marxians, Post Keynesians see production more as a Hobbesian rather than a Walrasian phenomenon, so that the employment contract is a power relationship, not just a set of mutually beneficial exchanges.

There is also a connection with New Keynesian ideas about "efficiency wages", since in both cases the "effort bargain" is taken very seriously indeed and is seen as a source of potential conflict as well as pro- viding evidence of "mutual gift exchange". Post Keynesians endorse the three New Keynesian principles set out by Joseph Stiglitz, who shows how, in the case of labour, "The Law of Supply and Demand has been repealed. The Law of the Single Price has been repealed. The Fundamental Theorem of Welfare Economics has been shown not to be valid" (Stiglitz 1987, p. 41). Labour markets do not clear because employers have no incentive to jeopardize the cooperation of their existing employees by accepting offers from outsiders to work at lower wages (note, however, that this complements the principle of effective demand; it does not replace it). Labour markets are segmented, in part because the positive relationship between wages and productivity dif- fers from firm to firm, so that workers with very similar characteristics (including "human capital" endowments) are paid very differently. And it is impossible to separate allocation and distribution, since feelings of fairness and justice influence the supply of effort and through it the level of production.

But there are other aspects to be taken into account when consider- ing the widening of wage differentials and the consequent increase in the inequality of income from employment that has been such a notable feature of the neoliberal era. Mainstream labour economists place most emphasis on technical change, which has increased the demand for highly skilled and educated labour at the expense of the low skilled. Post Keynesians place more emphasis on two additional factors: globalization, which has increased competition from produc- ers in low-wage developing countries and damaged the labour market position of unskilled workers in the advanced capitalist world, and (not unrelated to this) the far-reaching socio-political changes that have undermined the power of organized labour in the age of neoliberalism. Among the consequences of these changes are a decline in job security, a pronounced shift in the balance of labour market regulation in favour of employers and a long-run decline in the relative (and also in some cases, above all in the United States the absolute) value of the statutory minimum wage.

Something even more profound may be going on. Gerald Friedman (2014) has pointed to the rise of a "gig economy", in which a growing number of workers no longer have a "job" with a long-term connection to a company (and corresponding rights under common law and labour market legislation). Instead they are hired as supposedly independent contractors or "consultants", working like musicians on gigs to complete a specific task or for a (short) defined period of time. (Young academics struggling for work in the Australian university system know all about this). It undermines what is left of labour market regulation and shifts the burden of risk from companies to individuals and households in a process which, as Kurt Rothschild (1945) noted many years ago, makes a nonsense of the neoclassical notion that risk-bearing is a distinct input or "factor of production" supplied only by entrepreneurs. It is yet another consequence of the decline of the "stakeholder model" of the corporation in an age of finance-dominated capitalism (Slater and Spencer 2014).

There is also a macroeconomic dimension to the growth in inequality that has occurred in the last three to four decades. It concerns the shares of wages and profits in total output, which have defied Sidney Weintraub's expectations, not just in the United States but in almost all advanced capitalist countries. Far from remaining roughly constant, there has been a pronounced and continuing decline in the wage share and a corresponding increase in the share of profits, which has gone well beyond what was required to reverse the sharp but short-lived "profit squeeze" in the late 1960s and early 1970s. Neither the incoherent neoclassical marginal productivity theory of relative shares nor the Cambridge (UK) alternative to it that relies on changes in the ratio of investment to income offers a plausible explanation. The collapse of trade union bargaining power, which has been undermined by globalization, financialization and chronically high rates of unemployment, played (and continues to play) a crucial role in the declining wage share (Glyn 2006; Hein 2012, chapter 2).

Two points must be reiterated by way of conclusion. First, as we have just seen, Post Keynesian labour economics is inherently and unavoidably multi-disciplinary. The role of politics is inescapable, operating through the forces of globalization, financialization and the associated changes in class power and in social institutions. There are very clear links here with Marxian political economy and with institutionalism, which will be explored in Chapter 9. Second, detailed study of the labour market reinforces one of Thirlwall's core propositions (see Chapter 2). The level of employment is an essentially macroeconomic issue, so that microeconomic policy reforms (even if they operate in the right direction) will have a very limited impact on unemployment. The principle of effective demand is all-important.

The consumer and the household

The starting point, again, is fundamental uncertainty. Individuals cannot maximize their lifetime utility, subject to known budget constraints, since the available information is not adequate for this ambitious purpose, even probabilistically. This is not to say that people act irrationally, only that their rationality is bounded and they tend to opt for satisfactory rather than optimal outcomes (Simon 1991). Or, as Keynes put it, people behave reasonably, given the imperfect information at their disposal. There is one additional point to be made. The Post Keynesian approach to economic agency rejects both the methodological individualism of mainstream theory and the more extreme versions of methodological holism, according to which individual characteristics are entirely determined by the structure of society, in favour of an intermediate position in which agency and structure are mutually dependent. Thus consumer preferences are endogenous, to a certain extent, but individuals do enjoy some discretion, and they are not completely manipulated and exploited by corporate marketeers.

On the basis of these methodological considerations, Lavoie (2014, chapter 2) identifies seven principles of Post Keynesian consumer theory. The first is "procedural rationality", which involves the search for satisfactory rather than optimum outcomes; using the present and the recent past as guides to the future; following the opinions of the majority unless there are good reasons not to; attempting to reduce the amount of uncertainty, and deferring decisions when this proves impossible. Habits, routines, rules of thumb and conventions are all elements in what is better described as "reasonable", rather than rational, behaviour, as is the tendency to accept the opinions of others when there are no obvious grounds to reject them.

The second principle is that "needs are satiable": beyond a threshold level of consumption, no more of a good will be purchased, regardless of price, which casts doubt on the importance of the substitution effect that is emphasized in neoclassical demand theory. Third, "needs are separable": there is a hierarchy of needs, with elementary needs being satisfied first and higher-order needs only met subsequently to this. This permits consumers' decisions to be broken down into a series of smaller, multi-stage decisions. Again, however, it casts doubt on the principle of price substitution, since there may be little or no substitution between the categories of needs. There is considerable evidence that in many cases own- and cross-price elasticities of demand are very small.

This is closely related to the fourth principle, the "subordination of needs". The notion of a hierarchy of needs is a more elaborate version of the classical distinction between necessities and luxuries (and also the Sraffian distinction between "basic" and "non-basic" goods). It is consistent with procedural rationality, since there is no need for consumers to undertake a complete ordering of their preferences for all goods, but by the same token it rules out a single measure of utility and is inconsistent with the neoclassical principles of continuity of preferences, indifference and gross substitution. It implies that consumers have lexicographic preferences (Lavoie 2014, pp. 105–14).

The fifth principle is the "growth of needs": when the threshold level of one need has been satisfied, consumers move to needs situated on a higher plane, so long as their income level is sufficient. This implies that income effects are generally more important – perhaps much more important – than substitution effects. This, Lavoie notes, "is the microeconomic counterpart of the post-Keynesian focus on effective demand, that is, on macroeconomic income effects" (p. 102). Its salience has almost certainly increased in recent decades with the growth of consumer credit and household debt.

The sixth principle is "non-independence": individuals' tastes and preferences depend on the consumption decisions of others. We observe and imitate the choices of our friends and neighbours, and aspire to consume the goods already chosen by those slightly above us in the social hierarchy. All consumption is conspicuous, as institutional theorists from Thorstein Veblen to John Kenneth Galbraith (1958) have always insisted. This is closely related to the concept of positional goods, which are only perceived as being of value if other people do not consume them, since they would otherwise not give those who do a social cachet (Hirsch 1977). This seems to be a major factor in the well-known paradox of happiness: per capita real income rises over time, but happiness does not (Skidelsky and Skidelsky 2012).

Finally, there is the principle of "heredity", closely linked to the "endowment effect" noted by behavioural economists. Choices are not independent of the order in which they are made, and people dislike losing what they already have, even if they are being offered something better in exchange. This is another reason for believing that consumer preferences are endogenous and socially determined. All this – to repeat – provides an important link between Post Keynesian and institutionalist theory.

In addition, something must be said about gender issues and the household (Danby 2012). Labour is itself a produced input, though not a commodity produced for sale at a profit. Workers have to be fed and clothed in the short run, and reproduced in the long run. A household sector that produces these things can be added to a model of the production of traded commodities. In a broader sense, the category "household" might itself be regarded as a social and political construct, which is influenced by the law, by public policy and by government regulation. Downward causation, which was identified in the previous chapter as a significant influence on all economic relationships, is particularly important here.

One final point concerns the choice between work and leisure. In a well-known essay written and repeatedly rewritten between 1928 and 1930, Keynes discussed "the economic prospects for our grandchildren". He argued that mankind was solving its economic problem. Steady increases in the productivity of labour would, within a century, render scarcity a thing of the past and give rise to an age of leisure and abundance in which three hours of work per day would be sufficient to satisfy all human needs. In the future, Keynes believed, "the love of money . . . will be recognised for what it is, a somewhat disgusting morbidity, one of those semi-criminal, semi-pathological propensities which one hands over with a shudder to the specialists in mental disease" (Keynes 1930 [2008], pp. 23–4). As he knew, hours of work had indeed fallen substantially in the previous century, in a process that continued for another four decades after the appearance of his essay. Since the early 1970s, however, this decline has ceased, and even gone slightly into reverse, while the "love of money" shows no signs of disappearing. This is a striking conformation of the sixth principle of consumer theory, illustrating the social determination of individual tastes and the role of emulation in consumer choice (Stiglitz 2008). And it provides a link to the Post Keynesian approach to welfare economics.

The economics of welfare

When I travelled the world in late 1992, talking to Post Keynesian economists, I asked several of my interviewees for their opinions on the economics of welfare. William Milberg noted that, while there had been some criticism of the neoclassical approach to welfare, very little positive work had been done. Malcolm Sawyer doubted whether anything much could be said, given the emphasis that Post Keynesians placed on the endogeneity of tastes and preferences, which implied that notions of good and bad are in constant flux. And Peter Reynolds regarded the whole issue as secondary to the more important macroeconomic question of unemployment (King 1995a, pp. 61, 130–31, 149–50).

Very little had changed 20 years later, when Tae-Hee Jo concluded that "the Post Keynesian theory of welfare is still at an infant stage" (Jo 2012, p. 594). There would be general agreement that standards of welfare are (as Sawyer recognized) socially and historically conditioned, and that the nature of social agency was mis-specified in Paretian welfare economics, since the decisions of dominant agents (the state and large corporations) are much more influential than the choices of the great majority of individuals and households. Post Keynesians would also question the treatment of the state as benevolent and class-neutral – one assumption that Keynes shared with Pigou – and deny the usefulness of the concept of opportunity cost when capital and labour are both in excess supply.

But these are all essentially negative arguments, which offer little assistance on questions such as the appropriate level for a tax on carbon emissions (assuming that carbon pricing itself is accepted as a sensible means of combating global warming): should it be set at $20 a tonne or $120? Should tobacco taxes be increased by 50 per cent, as recommended in a recent report to the Australian government on the grounds that this would reduce cigarette consumption by 20 per cent and save many thousands of lives? If not, why not? If mainstream welfare economics is rejected, what should be put in its place to allow such questions to be answered?

One final question

In the "Concluding notes" to the *General Theory*, Keynes wrote that "if our central controls succeed in establishing an aggregate volume of output corresponding to full employment as nearly as is practicable, the classical theory comes into its own again from this point onwards" (Keynes 1936, p. 378). Remember here that by "classical theory" he meant the neoclassical microeconomic theory of Alfred Marshall and his disciples. Under full employment, Keynes continued, "there is no objection to be raised against the classical analysis of the manner in which private self-interest will determine what in particular is produced, in what proportions the factors of production will be combined to produce it, and how the value of the final product will be distributed between them". On the contrary: "I see no reason to suppose that the existing system seriously misemploys the factors of production that are in use" (pp. 378–9).

It is clear from the views that have been considered in this chapter that the majority of Post Keynesians would disagree with Keynes on this fundamental question, and would deny that what he termed the "Manchester System" of free market liberalism was the best system that could be found to produce the greatest happiness of the greatest number. One year after the publication of the *General Theory*, Joan Robinson produced a brief but trenchant critique of "the ideal system depicted in the textbooks of economics", in which "the free play of private enterprise, under competitive conditions, produced the maximum possible material welfare from the productive resources available to society" (Robinson 1937 [1970], p. 50). Given the very limited progress made in Post Keynesian welfare economics since 1937, it is just possible that the marginal intellectual return to microeconomics is higher today than the return to macroeconomics, and that substantially more Post Keynesian resources should be devoted to the former, and slightly fewer resources to the latter.

References

Andrews, P.W.S. 1949. *Manufacturing Business*, London: Macmillan.
Berle, A.A. Jr and G.C. Means. 1932. *The Modern Corporation and Private Property*, New York: Macmillan.
Coutts, K. and N. Norman. 2013. "Post-Keynesian approaches to industrial pricing: a survey and critique", in G.C. Harcourt and P. Kriesler (eds), *The Oxford Handbook of*

Post-Keynesian Economics, Volume 1: Theory and Origins, Oxford: Oxford University Press, pp. 443–66.

Danby, C. 2012. "Gender", in J.E. King (ed.), *The Elgar Companion to Post Keynesian Economics*, second edn, Cheltenham, UK and Northampton, MA, USA: Edward Elgar, pp. 250–54.

Eichner, A.S. 1975. *The Megacorp and Oligopoly: Micro Foundations of Macro Dynamics*, Cambridge: Cambridge University Press.

Eichner, A.S. 1987. *The Macrodynamics of Advanced Market Economies*, Armonk, NY: M.E. Sharpe.

Friedman, G. 2014. "Workers without employers: shadow corporations and the rise of the gig economy", *Review of Keynesian Economics*, **2**(2), Summer, 171–88.

Galbraith, J.K. 1958. *The Affluent Society*, Boston, MA: Houghton Mifflin.

Galbraith, J.K. 1967. *The New Industrial State*, Boston, MA: Houghton Mifflin.

Glyn, A. 2006. *Capitalism Unleashed: Finance, Globalization, and Welfare*, Oxford: Oxford University Press.

Harcourt, G.C. and P. Kenyon. 1976. "Pricing and the investment decision", *Kyklos*, **29**(3), 449–77.

Hein, E. 2012. *The Macroeconomics of Finance-dominated Capitalism – and Its Crisis*, Cheltenham, UK and Northampton, MA, USA: Edward Elgar.

Hirsch, F. 1977. *Social Limits to Growth*, London: Routledge & Kegan Paul.

Jo, T.-H. 2012. "Welfare economics", in J.E. King (ed.), *The Elgar Companion to Post Keynesian Economics*, second edn, Cheltenham, UK and Northampton, MA, USA: Edward Elgar, pp. 593–8.

Jo, T.-H. and Z. Todorova (eds). 2015. *Advancing the Frontiers of Heterodox Economics: Essays in Honor of Frederic Sterling Lee*, London and New York: Routledge.

Kalecki, M. 1937. "The principle of increasing risk", *Economica*, n.s., **4**(16), November, 440–47.

Kalecki, M. 1971. "Class struggle and the distribution of national income", *Kyklos*, **24**(1), 1–9.

Keynes, J.M. 1930. "Economic possibilities for our grandchildren", reprinted in L. Pecchi and G. Piga (eds) (2008), *Revisiting Keynes: Economic Possibilities for our Grandchildren*, Cambridge, MA: MIT Press, pp. 17–26.

Keynes, J.M. 1936. *The General Theory of Employment, Interest and Money*, London: Macmillan.

King, J.E. 1995a. *Conversations with Post Keynesians*, Basingstoke: Macmillan.

King, J.E. 1995b. "Outside the mainstream: Josef Steindl's *Economic Papers 1941–88*", *Cambridge Journal of Economics*, **19**(3), June, 463–75.

King, J.E. 2001. "Labour and unemployment", in R.P.F. Holt and S. Pressman (eds), *A New Guide to Post Keynesian Economics*, London and New York: Routledge, pp. 65–78.

Lavoie, M. 2014. *Post-Keynesian Economics: New Foundations*, Cheltenham, UK and Northampton, MA, USA: Edward Elgar.

Lee, F.S. 1998. *Post Keynesian Price Theory*, Cambridge: Cambridge University Press.

Lee, F.S. 2013. "Post-Keynesian price theory: from pricing to market governance to the economy as a whole", in G.C. Harcourt and P. Kriesler (eds), *The Oxford Handbook of*

Post-Keynesian Economics, Volume 1: Theory and Origins, Oxford: Oxford University Press, pp. 467–84.

Robinson, J. 1937. "The economic system in a socialist state", reprinted in E. Homberger, W. Janeways and S. Scharma (eds) (1970), *Ninety Years of the "Cambridge Review"*, London: Jonathan Cape, pp. 50–54.

Robinson, J. 1969. "Preface to the second edition" of J. Robinson, *The Economics of Imperfect Competition*, London: Macmillan, pp. v–xii (first published in 1933).

Rothschild, K.W. 1945. "Wages and risk-bearing", *Oxford Bulletin of Statistics*, 7(11–12), September, 193–8.

Simon, H.A. 1991. *Models of My Life*, New York: Basic Books.

Skidelsky, R. and E. Skidelsky. 2012. *How Much Is Enough? The Love of Money and the Case for the Good Life*, London: Allen Lane.

Slater, G. and D. Spencer. 2014. "Workplace relations, unemployment and finance-dominated capitalism", *Review of Keynesian Economics*, 2(2), Summer, 134–46.

Stiglitz, J.E. 1987. "The causes and consequences of the dependence of quality upon price", *Journal of Economic Literature*, 25(1), March, 1–48.

Stiglitz, J.E. 2008. "Towards a general theory of consumerism: reflections on Keynes's *Economic Possibilities for our Grandchildren*", in L. Pecchi and G. Piga (eds), *Revisiting Keynes: Economic Possibilities for our Grandchildren*, Cambridge, MA: MIT Press, pp. 41–85.

Sylos-Labini, P. 1961. *Oligopoly and Technical Progress*, Cambridge, MA: Harvard University Press.

Szego, A. 1991. "The logic of a shortage economy: a critique of Kornai from a Kaleckian macroeconomic perspective", *Journal of Post Keynesian Economics*, 13(3), Spring, 328–36.

Wood, A. 1975. *A Theory of Profits*, Cambridge: Cambridge University Press.

6 Economic growth, development and the world economy

The Harrod growth model

In the *General Theory* Keynes had allowed for positive net investment but held the capital stock constant, and in his review of the book A.C. Pigou had criticized him for the inconsistency (Pigou 1936). The first generation of Keynes's Cambridge disciples spent the next quarter of a century developing a theory of economic growth – "generalising the *General Theory*" to the long run, as Joan Robinson described it (Harcourt 2006). The resulting Post Keynesian theory of growth had strong similarities with the model of "expanded reproduction" sketched by Marx in volume II of *Capital* and subsequently elaborated on by socialist theorists like G.A. Feldman and Michał Kalecki (Dobb 1973, pp. 226–40; Sardoni 2013). In the United States, an important contribution was made by the Russian-born growth theorist Evsey Domar (1957).

The first substantial steps towards a Post Keynesian theory of growth were, however, taken by the Oxford economist (and first biographer of Keynes), Roy Harrod, who made a crucial distinction between three rates of growth: the actual growth rate (G), the "warranted" rate (G_w), which leaves entrepreneurs satisfied with their productive capacity, and the "natural" or maximum possible rate (G_n). Harrod noted that there was no reason to expect the three growth rates to be equal, and that this was a major source of potential economic instability.

Harrod's actual rate of growth is defined as $G = s/C$, where $s = S/Y$ is the proportion of income that is saved, and $C = \Delta K/\Delta Y$ is the desired incremental (or marginal) capital–output ratio. Despite Harrod's slightly misleading algebra, growth in his model is driven by business investment decisions (and hence by the expected profitability of additions to the stock of capital, Keynes's "marginal efficiency of capital"), not by decisions to save. The desired incremental capital–output ratio is principally determined by technology, although

Harrod allowed for it also to be "somewhat dependent" on the rate of interest. On the (provisional) assumption that C is constant and equal to 4, and with 10 per cent of output devoted to net investment, the actual rate of growth would be 2.5 per cent per annum (Harrod 1939, pp. 16–17).

Now consider the relationship between the actual and the warranted rates of growth. If G exceeds G_w, the actual capital–output ratio will be less than entrepreneurs desire, so they will increase investment and thereby further increase the actual growth rate, widening the gap between G and G_w. The reverse process will occur if G falls below G_w. "A departure from equilibrium, instead of being self-righting, will be self-aggravating. G_w represents a moving equilibrium, but a highly unstable one" (p. 22). In the Harrod model a capitalist economy is precariously balanced on a knife-edge (though Harrod himself disliked the term).

The Old Keynesian response to this problem was touched on in Chapter 2. In the Solow–Swan growth model there is a smooth, monotonic, twice-differentiable production function relating output to the capital stock, and output per unit of labour to the capital–labour ratio. The rate of interest is determined by the marginal product of capital, and the incremental capital–output ratio (Harrod's C) is a variable, not a constant. It is determined by capital–labour substitution undertaken by entrepreneurs in response to changes in the relative prices of the two factors, themselves determined by the marginal productivities of labour and capital. Over-investment depresses the rate of interest and increases the equilibrium (or "warranted") value of C, eliminating the gap between G and G_w.

Grave doubt was cast on this neoclassical substitution mechanism by the Cambridge controversies in the theory of capital (Harcourt 1972). Early Post Keynesian attempts to overcome the knife-edge instability problem held C constant but allowed for variability in the saving ratio s. This was assumed to be a consequence of changes in the relative income shares of capital, whose owners had a high savings propensity, and labour, with a much lower propensity to save, perhaps as low as zero (Kaldor 1956).

But this did not address the second problem that Harrod had identified, with respect to the "natural" or maximum rate of growth (G_n), which was equal to the sum of the growth rates of the labour force and of labour productivity. Probably G_n is better characterized as the full employment rate of growth, since if the actual rate of growth falls below the natural rate, full employment cannot be maintained. In Post Keynesian growth theory there is no presumption that labour will be fully employed, even in the long run: everything depends on the relationship between aggregate supply and aggregate demand, that is, on the principle of effective demand. Assume, however, that we do start from a position of full employment. Then, if the labour force grows at 1.5 per cent per annum, and output per hour worked grows at 1 per cent, G_n will equal 2.5 per cent. The actual growth rate cannot exceed 2.5 per cent. If it falls below 2.5 per cent, involuntary unemployment will result.

In Post Keynesian growth theory, capital–labour substitution cannot be relied upon to restore full employment, as it is in neoclassical theory. Government action of some sort will be required, even in the long run: monetary policy, perhaps, or fiscal policy, or that "somewhat comprehensive socialization of investment" that Keynes had mooted in the *General Theory*. Joan Robinson described the unlikely situation in which stable growth with full employment occurred (so that $G = G_w = G_n$) as a "golden age", by which she meant that it was both desirable and highly unlikely to occur in practice (Robinson 1956, pp. 99–100). The exceptional period 1945–73, in which full employment actually did prevail in most advanced capitalist countries for most of the time, came to be known as the "golden age of capitalism" (Marglin and Schor 1990). It has not been repeated, even in the alleged "Great Moderation" between 1992 and 2007, when unemployment was persistently higher than it had been in the earlier period, in almost all advanced capitalist countries.

Some complications

This Harrod (or Harrod–Domar) model is the simplest possible version of the Post Keynesian theory of economic growth. It rests on three simplifying assumptions, which later theorists have attempted to remove. First, technical progress is exogenous; that is to say, determined outside the system by the non-economic forces of science and technology. Second, there is only one good, so that we do not need to distinguish between capital goods and consumption goods, and even the rather basic distinction between the primary, secondary and tertiary sectors of the economy can be ignored. Third, the economy is closed, so that foreign trade and international capital movements have nothing to do with economic growth. I shall relax each assumption in turn.

Post Keynesian thinking on endogenous technical change began with Nicholas Kaldor (1957), whose first growth model involved explicit direct criticism of the Solow–Swan approach. Kaldor refused to accept the neoclassical distinction between changes in techniques of production caused by an increase in the capital–labour ratio with given technology and those induced by technological change. New technology normally needs to be embodied in new capital equipment, he argued, and a higher capital–labour ratio generally involves new technology. Hence there is no basis for a distinction between movements along a given production function and shifts in that function due to technical change. This is a "vintage model" of the capital stock, but (unlike wine) the newer, the better.

Kaldor replaced the neoclassical aggregate production with a Technical Progress Function that relates the rate of growth of output per worker to the rate of growth of capital per worker. Thus technical progress becomes endogenous: it depends on the ratio of investment to income (that is, on Harrod's s). Five years later Kaldor went one step further, eliminating the notion of capital altogether from the analysis. The rate of growth of productivity is now determined by the rate of growth of investment per worker, not by the rate of growth of capital per worker (Kaldor and Mirrlees 1962). Again, all this is quite openly anti-neoclassical: there is no capital–labour substitution induced by changes in relative factor prices, no aggregate production functions, no diminishing returns. And Say's Law is stood on its head, since demand now creates its own supply.

Kaldor's ideas have been taken up (sometimes with due acknowledgement) by neoclassical growth theorists in the so-called "new growth theory". Ironically, it can be shown that the AK or constant returns to capital version of new growth theory is none other than the Harrod growth equation. Totally differentiating $Y = AK$ and then dividing by Y gives $dY/Y = AdK/Y = AI/Y$, or $G = s/C$, where $I/Y = s$ and $A = 1/C$. In the AK model, A is simply the inverse of the incremental capital–output ratio (Thirlwall 2013, p. 38).

There is an additional and more interesting conclusion: endogenous technical change implies that G_n is no longer independent of either G or G_w, so that the Harrod knife-edge problem may be less acute than it initially appeared to be (Setterfield 2013, pp. 246–9). Empirical evidence to support the interdependence of the three growth rates came from Verdoorn's Law, in which (as early as 1949) the Belgian economist P.J. Verdoorn identified a positive relationship between the rate of growth of labour productivity and the rate of growth of output, confirming the existence of dynamic increasing returns to scale. Endogenous technical change is perhaps the most obvious explanation of the Verdoorn relationship, but it is not the only reason to expect the maximum rate of growth to be a function of the actual growth rate. The rate of growth of the labour force will also increase, perhaps due to faster population growth and almost certainly also as a result of the higher labour force participation rates that are induced by more rapid growth of output, and hence of the demand for labour.

This is a notable instance of the phenomenon of path dependence, or hysteresis, in which the equilibrium position is not fixed, but instead moves as the economy moves towards it. And path dependence works in both directions. Lower output means lower potential output, and slower growth of actual output leads to a lower potential growth rate, as seems to have been the case in the Great Recession that began in 2008. Laurence Ball (2014) uses mainstream estimates of potential output by the Organisation for Economic Co-operation and Development (OECD) and International Monetary Fund (IMF) to calculate the losses in potential output for OECD member nations. In the hardest hit countries (Greece, Hungary and Ireland), these losses exceeded 30 per cent, and were continuing to depress the growth rate of potential output.

Reduced investment and the resulting reduction in the capital stock (and increase in its average age) was the most important causal factor, followed by the effects on the labour force. Ball suggests one further source of endogeneity, this time a financial one: tighter credit rationing makes it harder for new small enterprises to be established, and this discourages innovation. In addition to the long-run consequences, there are also short-run ramifications of hysteresis: the NAIRU (Non-Accelerating Inflation Rate of Unemployment) is a positive function of the actual unemployment rate, and is not, as the monetarists maintain, in any sense a "natural" rate of unemployment.

Verdoorn's Law was intended to apply only to manufacturing, not to agriculture or services. Reflecting on the relatively slow growth of the British economy, relative to France, Italy and West Germany in two decades after 1945, Kaldor concluded that one-sector growth models were not appropriate. His "first growth law" states that there is a strong causal relation between the rate of growth of manufacturing output and the rate of growth of GDP: manufacturing is the engine of growth, in a way that agriculture and services cannot be (Thirlwall 2013, p. 43). Half a century ago Kaldor's law was almost certainly true in this simple form, but it probably needs reformulation for the greatly changed conditions of 2015, to include a distinction between low-tech and high-tech manufacturing and some allowance for the operation of dynamic increasing returns to scale in the large and growing information technology component of the tertiary sector. Post Keynesians would be wise to remember that Apple, Google and Microsoft are now the first, second and fourth largest corporations, by total share value, in the world. At the time of writing (December 2014) Exxon had slipped from second to third place; there were no manufacturing companies in the top four.

Structural change plays an even more important role in other versions of Post Keynesian growth theory. Indeed, it can be argued that the role of historical, institutional, social and political forces is such that in principle there can be no single general Post Keynesian theory of growth (Kriesler 2013, pp. 539–40). The two most influential variants of the structural analysis of growth are Edward Nell's model of "transformational growth" (Nell 1998) and Luigi Pasinetti's multi-sectoral analysis of structural economic dynamics (Pasinetti 1993, 2007). In both models, the connections to Marxian political economy are evident. And the emphasis on innovation and entrepreneurship recalls the work of Joseph Schumpeter and suggests strong links to institutionalist and evolutionary thought. These affinities will be further explored in Chapter 9.

Relaxing the third simplifying assumption requires us to take account of the open economy aspects of economic growth. Again, Kaldor must be our starting point. Reflecting on the poor growth performance of the British economy in the third quarter of the twentieth century, he managed to convince himself that exports are the only truly exogenous source of demand, since consumption and government expenditure depend on income, and investment depends directly (via the accelerator mechanism) on the growth of consumption and hence indirectly upon income (Kaldor 1966). There is no need to go quite this far in order to accept that, for a small open economy, the rate of growth of demand for the country's exports is a major determinant of its overall growth rate.

This insight has been formalized into a model of balance of payments-constrained growth, which dynamizes Harrod's 1933 foreign trade multiplier in the form of what has come to be known as Thirlwall's Law (McCombie and Thirlwall 1994). Where g_b is the balance of payments-constrained growth rate, ε is the world's income-elasticity of demand for the country's exports, π is its own income-elasticity of demand for imports and z is the rate of growth of world income, the Law in its simplest form states that $g_b = \varepsilon z/\pi = x/\pi$, where x (= εz) is the rate of growth of exports (see Thirlwall 2013, chapter 5 for a more elaborate formulation). The insight behind the Law is that growth is constrained by the need for expenditure on imports not to grow faster than the foreign currency received from exports. Sensitivity analysis reveals that allowing for capital imports eases the constraint only slightly (Thirlwall 2013, pp. 106–7).

In the pre-1973 world of fixed exchange rates the balance of payments constraint was obvious, and in the British case it was implemented through the recurrent deflationary fiscal and monetary policies that were imposed in order to "save the pound", and which generated a "stop–go" cycle that inhibited growth (Dow 1964). Since the collapse of the Bretton Woods system, currency depreciation offers some respite, but there is considerable evidence that in the long run (or perhaps the very long run) the balance of payments constraint cannot be avoided through continuous currency depreciation (Blecker 2013, pp. 394–6). In the medium term, the slightly different version of Kaldor's insights represented by the "export-led cumulative causation" model seems to perform rather better (pp. 403–8). Both models suggest the need to include export demand and path dependency in any realistic Post Keynesian theory of economic growth.

Economic development

Given the importance of history, institutions and social and political forces in the Post Keynesian approach to growth, it follows that a specific economics of development is needed to understand the particular problems faced by poor countries in their attempt to catch up with the advanced capitalist world. Both Kaldor and Kalecki found clear similarities between the experience of today's rich countries in the early stages of their industrialization and the circumstances of the poor countries today. As Kaldor told a Chinese audience in 1956, unemployment in nineteenth-century Europe was largely (as Marx described it) the consequence of a permanent shortage of capital, rather than the result of a chronic deficiency of effective demand, and the solution involved a massive increase in investment, rather than Keynesian demand management policies (Kaldor 1960). What Kalecki described as "the tragedy of investment" in advanced capitalist countries – it raises effective demand but also increases the capital stock and thereby reduces the scope for future investment – does not apply in developing economies, where investment can be undertaken almost without limit and does not represent a "double-edged sword" (Kalecki 1960; Kriesler 2013, pp. 541–4).

It appears to be the case that all three of Kaldor's growth laws apply to developing countries. Thirlwall cites studies of 45 African countries, 28 regions of China and seven Latin American nations. In all three cases, there was evidence of a strong positive causal relationship between the growth of manufacturing output and the growth of GDP; between the growth of manufacturing output and labour productivity growth in manufacturing (Verdoorn's Law); and between the growth of the manufacturing sector and the growth of labour productivity outside manufacturing, as labour is withdrawn from low-productivity employment in agriculture and the petty service sector (Thirlwall 2013, pp. 43–50)

The maximum or "natural" rate of growth is endogenous in developing countries, even more so than in advanced capitalist economies. There is considerable evidence of this for Latin America (pp. 63–70). This is due to the much greater prevalence of unemployment and underemployment in developing economies, and the much greater scope for migration of labour from the countryside to the towns. The Lewis model, in which the rate of migration is the most important factor in the process of development, is entirely consistent with Post Keynesian thinking on these issues (Kriesler 2013, pp. 544–8). It implies that "demand creates its own supply, within limits" (Thirlwall 2013, p. 70), so that differences in growth rates between countries depend to a considerable extent on differences in the strength of demand, and in particular on the constraints on demand. The two most pressing constraints in developing countries are balance of payments difficulties and domestic supply bottlenecks (for example, in the supply of food and basic raw materials), which cause inflation.

There is a clear affinity between Post Keynesian thinking on the problems of economic development and the "structuralist" school of thought inspired by Raul Prebisch, who drew on the experience of

Latin America and above all on his native Argentina. As the name implies, Latin American structuralism emphasized the structural differences between rich and poor countries, in particular the relative importance of manufacturing as opposed to primary production and the resulting difference in the income-elasticity of demand for exports. It served as an inspiration for subsequent models of economic development constrained by the balance of payments, which forecast that the gap between rich and poor countries would increase over time. Today the resulting "centre–periphery" models are more commonly referred to as "North–South" models, as the notion of a "Global South" (much of it located north of the equator) became popular (Dutt 2002). They are also sometimes presented in terms of a distinction between OECD and non-OECD nations.

However, the central message of this "Post Keynesian-cum-structuralist approach" (Blankenburg and Palma 2012, p. 139) remains the same. "Long-run growth of the world economy is determined by demand in the North, and in long-run equilibrium there is uneven development in the sense that northern capital and output grow at a faster rate than southern capital and output because the import elasticity of the North is less than that of the South" (Thirlwall 2013, p. 109). The basic model can be extended to allow for a continuum of goods produced in the South, from very basic to relatively high-tech, and to take account of long-term capital movements, the burden of debt and the benefits of debt relief (Vera 2006). Thirlwall's summary table of relevant empirical studies cites 42 papers and is spread over four pages (Thirlwall 2013, pp. 112–15).

The policy implications are profound. Again Thirlwall provides a succinct summary of the evidence on the effects of trade liberalization in the developing world. Free trade appears to raise income per capita, but not to increase the rate of growth of income. The impact of trade liberalization on world poverty has been minimal, and it has actually made the global distribution of income less equal, both by widening the gap between rich and poor countries and by increasing wage differentials between unskilled workers in poor countries and everyone else in all countries (not just in the developed countries, as the Samuelson–Stolper theorem would suggest). Finally, there is no clear evidence that the liberalizing countries have done better, overall, than those that failed to liberalize (Thirlwall 2013, chapter 6).

Thus Post Keynesians reject the IMF's insistence on financial and trade liberalization and on currency depreciation in developing countries, on the grounds that these measures will often exacerbate the balance of payments constraints on growth and give rise to sharp and destabilizing movements in exchange rates. Financial liberalization often produced instability and crises rather than financial deepening and faster rates of output growth, even before the Global Financial Crisis of 2007–08. Thus there is a strong case for international capital controls, at least over short-time capital movements, and for some degree of control over exchange rates (Stallings and Studart 2005).

International economics

The Post Keynesian critique of the neoclassical theory of comparative advantage is not restricted to developing economies. There are three fundamental objections, which are relevant also to the advanced capitalist world. First, the theory assumes that there is no involuntary unemployment, which is clearly false all the time in almost all poor countries, and has not been true in the developed capitalist economies since the end of the "golden age" in the early 1970s. Second, it assumes automatic, rapid and painless balance of payments adjustments, via changes in exchange rates and/or capital movements, so that money does not matter, in international as in domestic macroeconomic theory. Third, its treatment of the gains from trade is purely static, focussing on the adoption of a new international division of labour with given production functions and unchanging technology.

The third objection is especially powerful. Post Keynesians emphasize that the dynamic gains from trade are quantitatively much more important than the static benefits. These gains from trade involve changes in elements that are held constant in neoclassical trade theory: improvements in the flow of ideas, new knowledge, investment and economies of scale – above all, the dynamic external economies of scale that lie behind Kaldor's second and third growth laws. This suggests that absolute advantage is often more important than comparative advantage (Milberg 1994). It also provides a strong case for infant industry protection, which was in fact practised by all today's rich countries while they were in the early stages of their own industrialization (Chang 2002). Although protection is inconsistent with the free trade precepts of the Washington Consensus, it is advocated by Post Keynesians and also by some prominent New Keynesians, like Paul Krugman and Joseph Stiglitz (2006, p. 72, cited by Thirlwall 2013, p. 128).

Again, Thirlwall surveys the extensive evidence on all these questions, with particular reference to Latin America (Thirlwall 2013, pp. 133–41). His conclusion would be endorsed by the great majority of Post Keynesian development economists:

> In the final analysis, structural change which adds to the demand for domestically produced tradable goods is the only way that poor developing countries can grow faster on a sustainable basis. The market mechanism by itself is unlikely to bring about the required structural change without help from the state. (Thirlwall 2013, p. 156)

And this reinforces the case for managed exchange rates. International capital flows are "active" and "autonomous" and depend on investors' portfolio decisions. They are not "transitory factors, serving merely to finance trade flows". Thus exchange rates are not set in "a market characterized by stability, efficiency and optimality", but rather by a market in which "agents' imperfectly considered actions create currency prices" (Harvey 2012, pp. 186, 188). Once again, the financial liberalization demanded by the Washington Consensus cannot be relied upon to produce optimal outcomes.

Some methodological conclusions

We might conclude by considering the broader methodological implications of the Post Keynesian approach to the problems of growth and development. First and foremost is the significance of path dependence, hysteresis and circular and cumulative causation, and the need to take account of historical (as opposed to analytical) time (Robinson 1962, pp. 23–6). Mark Setterfield distinguishes "weak" and "strong" versions of path dependence. The former refers to the sensitivity of an economy's growth path to initial conditions, while the latter suggests the need to allow for a series of "growth regimes", in which institutional, social and political change is inextricably bound up with the process of economic growth. Setterfield distinguishes the "golden age" (1945–73) from the "age of decline" that followed it (1973–89) and the subsequent "financialised growth regime" that began c.1990. This final growth regime culminated in the global financial crisis of 2007–08, ushering in the "Great Recession" that continues to constrain economic growth in almost all the rich countries (Setterfield 2013, pp. 243–6). This is an application of the "evolutionary Keynesianism" advocated by John Cornwall and Wendy Cornwall (2001), and it casts doubt on any simple equilibrium approach to the analysis of economic growth.

Second, the role of investment (and thus of effective demand) in all Post Keynesian growth theories suggests that no sharp distinction can be drawn between short-period and long-period analysis. The same forces operate in both cases, and Kalecki was right to see the long run as having no independent existence: "the long-run trend is but a slowly changing component of a chain of short-period situations; it has no independent entity [existence?]" (Kalecki 1971, p. 165). Thus Post Keynesian growth models have always been models of unstable, cyclical growth, from the earliest efforts of Roy Harrod to connect the Keynesian multiplier with the accelerator principle to produce a theory of the trade cycle (Harrod 1936), to Richard Goodwin's use of the Lotka–Volterra predator–prey model in the 1960s (Blatt 1983), right through to the most sophisticated use of computer simulation to model Minskyian debt dynamics in the context of growth (Keen 2013). This, Steve Keen concludes, is "the stylized fact that distinguishes the Post Keynesian approach to growth theory from the neoclassical models" (Keen 2012, p. 275).

And there is one final methodological implication. For Post Keynesian growth theorists, formal modelling is not sufficient, as the repeated insistence on the role of institutions, politics and history makes very clear. But it does appear to be necessary, if the profound insights of Harrod, Kaldor, Robinson and the other pioneers are to be used effectively to understand the complex and difficult world that we actually live in.

References

Ball, L. 2014. "Long-term damage from the Great Recession in OECD countries", *European Journal of Economics and Economic Policies: Intervention*, **11**(2), 149–60.

Blankenburg, S. and G. Palma. 2012. "Economic development", in J.E. King (ed.), *The Elgar Companion to Post Keynesian Economics*, second edn, Cheltenham, UK and Northampton, MA, USA: Edward Elgar, pp. 138–43.

Blatt, J. 1983. *Dynamic Economic Systems: A Post Keynesian Approach*, Armonk, NY: M.E. Sharpe.

Blecker, R. 2013. "Long-run growth in open economies: export-led cumulative causation or a balance-of-payments constraint?", in G.C. Harcourt and P. Kriesler (eds), *The Oxford Handbook of Post-Keynesian Economics, Volume 1: Theory and Origins*, Oxford: Oxford University Press, pp. 390–414.

Chang, H.-J. 2002. *Kicking Away the Ladder: Development Strategy in Historical Perspective*, London: Anthem Press.

Cornwall, J. and W. Cornwall. 2001. *Capitalist Development in the Twentieth Century: An Evolutionary Keynesian Analysis*, Cambridge: Cambridge University Press.

Dobb, M.H. 1973. *Theories of Value and Distribution since Adam Smith: Ideology and Economic Theory*, Cambridge: Cambridge University Press.

Domar, E.D. 1957. *Essays in the Theory of Economic Growth*, Oxford: Oxford University Press.

Dow, J.C.R. 1964. *The Management of the British Economy 1945–60*, Cambridge: Cambridge University Press.

Dutt, A.K. 2002. "Thirlwall's law and uneven development", *Journal of Post Keynesian Economics*, **24**(3), Spring, 367–90.

Harcourt, G.C. 1972. *Some Cambridge Controversies in the Theory of Capital*, Cambridge: Cambridge University Press.

Harcourt, G.C. 2006. *The Structure of Post-Keynesian Economics: The Core Contributions of the Pioneers*, Cambridge: Cambridge University Press.

Harrod, R. 1936. *The Trade Cycle*, Oxford: Clarendon Press.

Harrod, R.F. 1939. "An essay in dynamic theory", *Economic Journal*, **49**(193), March, 14–33.

Harvey, J.T. 2012. "Exchange rates", in J.E. King (ed.), *The Elgar Companion to Post Keynesian Economics*, second edn, Cheltenham, UK and Northampton, MA, USA: Edward Elgar, pp. 185–9.

Kaldor, N. 1956. "Alternative theories of distribution", *Review of Economic Studies*, **23**(2), 83–100.

Kaldor, N. 1957. "A model of economic growth", *Economic Journal*, **67**(268), December, 591–624.

Kaldor, N. 1960. "Capitalist evolution in the light of Keynesian economics", in N. Kaldor, *Essays on Economic Stability and Growth*, London: Duckworth, pp. 242–58.

Kaldor, N. 1966. *Causes of the Slow Rate of Economic Growth of the United Kingdom: An Inaugural Lecture*, Cambridge: Cambridge University Press.

Kaldor, N. and J. Mirrlees. 1962. "A new model of economic growth", *Review of Economic Studies*, **29**(3), June, 174–92.

Kalecki, M. 1960. "Unemployment in underdeveloped countries", *Indian Journal of Labour Economics*, **3**(2), July, 59–61, reprinted in J. Osiatynski (ed.) (1993), *The Collected Works of Michał Kalecki. Volume 5: Developing Economies*, Oxford: Clarendon Press, pp. 3–5.

Kalecki, M. 1971. *Selected Essays on the Dynamics of the Capitalist Economy*, Cambridge: Cambridge University Press.

Keen, S. 2012. "Growth theory", in J.E. King (ed.), *The Elgar Companion to Post Keynesian Economics*, second edn, Cheltenham, UK and Northampton, MA, USA: Edward Elgar, pp. 271–7.

Keen, S. 2013. "A monetary Minsky model of the Great Moderation and the Great Recession", *Journal of Economic Behavior and Organization*, **86**, February, 221–35.

Kriesler, P. 2013. "Post Keynesian perspectives on economic development and growth", in G.C. Harcourt and P. Kriesler (eds), *The Oxford Handbook of Post-Keynesian*

Economics, Volume 1: Theory and Origins, Oxford: Oxford University Press, pp. 539–55.

Marglin, S. and J. Schor (eds). 1990. *The Golden Age of Capitalism: Reinterpreting the Postwar Experience*, Oxford: Clarendon Press.

McCombie, J.S.L. and A.P. Thirlwall. 1994. *Economic Growth and the Balance-of-payments Constraint*, Basingstoke: Macmillan.

Milberg, W. 1994. "Is absolute advantage passé? Towards a Post Keynesian/Marxian theory of international trade", in M. Glick (ed.), *Competition, Technology and Money: Classical and Post-Keynesian Perspectives*, Aldershot, UK and Brookfield, VT, USA: Edward Elgar, pp. 220–36.

Nell, E.J. 1998. *The General Theory of Transformational Growth*, Cambridge: Cambridge University Press.

Pasinetti, L.L. 1993. *Structural Economic Dynamics*, Cambridge: Cambridge University Press.

Pasinetti, L.L. 2007. *Keynes and the Cambridge Keynesians: A "Revolution in Economics" to be Accomplished*, Cambridge: Cambridge University Press.

Pigou, A.C. 1936. "Mr J.M. Keynes's general theory of employment, interest and money", *Economica* n.s., May, 115–32.

Robinson, J. 1956. *The Accumulation of Capital*, London: Macmillan.

Robinson, J. 1962. *Essays in the Theory of Economic Growth*, London: Macmillan.

Sardoni, C. 2013. "Marx and the Post-Keynesians", in G.C. Harcourt and P. Kriesler (eds), *The Oxford Handbook of Post-Keynesian Economics, Volume 2: Critiques and Methodology*, Oxford: Oxford University Press, pp. 231–44.

Setterfield, M. 2013. "Endogenous growth: a Kaldorian approach", in G.C. Harcourt and P. Kriesler (eds), *The Oxford Handbook of Post-Keynesian Economics, Volume 1: Theory and Origins*, Oxford: Oxford University Press, pp. 231–56.

Stallings, B. and R. Studart. 2005. *Finance for Development: Latin America in Comparative Perspective*, Washington, DC: Brookings Institution Press.

Stiglitz, J.E. 2006. *Making Globalization Work*, New York: Norton.

Thirlwall, A.P. 2013. *Economic Growth in an Open Developing Economy: The Role of Structure and Demand*, Cheltenham, UK and Northampton, MA, USA: Edward Elgar.

Vera, L.A. 2006. "The balance of payments constrained growth model; a North–South approach", *Journal of Post Keynesian Economics*, **29**(1), Fall, 367–90.

7 Why it all matters: economic policy

Post Keynesian politics

Keynes was never greatly interested in economic theory for its own sake, and instead regarded economics as a policy science, or perhaps as an art. Post Keynesians share these practical concerns, and have developed a distinctive approach to both the targets and the instruments of macroeconomic policy. Thus their views on a very wide range of economic policy questions differentiate them very clearly from the mainstream, and they have not forgotten the classic advice of Jan Tinbergen (1956): make use of at least as many policy instruments as you have policy targets, but do not attach specific instruments rigidly to particular targets.

Post Keynesians advocate four targets, or policy objectives: full employment; a low but positive inflation rate; a fair distribution of income and wealth; and financial stability. The third and fourth objectives are entirely ignored by the mainstream, and the first features only indirectly, through the gap between actual and potential output; a specific numerical unemployment target is rarely mentioned. Accordingly, Post Keynesians need a significantly wider range of policy instruments than the mainstream (Arestis 2013). I shall discuss these instruments under five headings: monetary policy; fiscal policy; prices and incomes policy; international economic policy issues; and environmental policies.

First, however, something needs to be said about politics. Do Post Keynesians really share a common political position? I think it would be generally agreed that, as a general rule, they are left of centre, more so today than previous generations were. (The political centre has, of course, shifted a long way to the right in the last 40 years.) Keynes himself was – to a rather limited extent – a man of the left, though just how far to the left remains a matter of contention. His biographer refers approvingly to Keynes's "middle way" (Skidelsky 2009, chapter 7), and he himself described the political implications of the *General Theory* as being "moderately conservative" (Keynes 1936, p. 377).

The first generation of Cambridge Post Keynesians were all social democrats of one sort or another, with Joan Robinson's fascination with Mao's China distinguishing her from Nicholas Kaldor, a middle-of-the-road Labour Party man who shifted slightly to the left in his old age as a reaction to Margaret Thatcher. In the United States Sidney Weintraub and Hyman Minsky were both liberal Democrats, and Paul Davidson remains one. This was almost a centrist position in the 1960s, but has much more radical connotations half a century later, when Barack Obama, choosing his economic advisers in 2009, found even New Keynesians like Paul Krugman and Joseph Stiglitz too radical for his liking. Subsequent generations of Post Keynesians on both sides of the Atlantic have tended towards reformist social democracy, while the Kaleckians have some sympathy with Michał Kalecki's undogmatic version of Marxian political economy.

There are good reasons for this affinity with the left. Keynes wrote the *General Theory* in the firm belief that the capitalist system was in need of fundamental reform. This was understandably a very common view in the 1930s, and was shared by many who were less critical of "classical" macroeconomics than he was: take a look at A.C. Pigou's *Socialism Versus Capitalism* if you doubt this statement (Pigou 1937). Post Keynesians have always insisted on the need for systematic regulation of markets – above all, vigilant regulation of financial markets – on the grounds that market failure is generally more dangerous than state failure. In the age of neoliberalism (unlike in the 1930s) this alone is sufficient to place them some way to the left of the majority of the profession.

The Post Keynesian concern with questions of the distribution of income and wealth also needs to be emphasized. In part this reflects a concern for social justice, and in part it is simply an inescapable consequence of the abandonment of the marginal productivity theory of relative income shares. This entails a rejection of the ethical justification for profits that was developed by J.B. Clark, according to which the owners of capital deserve to receive a reward for their contribution to production no less than the suppliers of labour power. The Cambridge controversies in the theory of capital muddied these apologetic waters for all eternity.

For Post Keynesians, there is also an inescapable macroeconomic dimension. The first principle of an acceptable distribution of income is that it maintains macroeconomic stability, so that it is consistent with full employment without demand inflation. Given that poor people tend to spend a larger proportion of their incomes than rich people, there is a presumption in favour of greater equality in the personal distribution of income, and a strong case for a stable or increasing wage share in GDP. In the concluding chapter to the *General Theory* Keynes himself admitted as much (Keynes 1936, pp. 372–6). This reinforces the underlying egalitarianism of many Post Keynesians, and strengthens the arguments in favour of strongly progressive income (or expenditure) taxation and generous welfare payments, especially to families with children (Pressman 2014).

Monetary policy

The underlying theoretical propositions that guide Post Keynesian thinking on monetary policy were summarized in Chapters 2–3: opposition to Say's Law and the classical dichotomy; insistence on the endogeneity of money; rejection of the loanable funds theory of interest and the associated notion of a "natural" rate of interest; recognition of the fragility of the financial system and the need to be constantly alert to the consequences of financial innovation.

Thus the first generation of Post Keynesians were strongly critical of monetarism, both as a theory and as a set of policy proposals. Since money was endogenous, they argued, the direction of causation was the reverse of that claimed by Friedman and the Chicago school. Inflation originated in the "real" economy, in the product market and especially in the markets for labour and raw materials. Attempts to combat inflation by implementing a rigid rule for the growth of the money supply would not succeed, but (through the associated fiscal austerity, high interest rates and overvalued exchange rates) they would inflict serious damage on output and employment (Kaldor 1982). Monetarism was "the incomes policy of Karl Marx" (Balogh 1982, p. 77), which used the reserve army of the unemployed to keep the power of organized labour in check and to preserve discipline in the factories.

There was also an important point of political principle involved in the Post Keynesian critique of monetarism: monetary policy should be subject to democratic control in the interests of the great majority, and not placed in the hands of supposedly "independent" central banks that in practice remained very much dependent on the tiny, very rich minority of players in the financial markets. In fact, as Pixley et al. (2013) suggest, central banks have always been embedded in economic and political coalitions and conflicts, so that the term "independence" can never be used without significant qualification. What is often mistakenly described as central bank "independence" should instead be understood as a different form of dependence, on the coalition of interests that supported the deregulation of the global financial system before the onset of the Global Financial Crisis in 2007–08 (see Chapter 8). In effect the move to central bank "independence" in the 1990s was a form of disguised privatization (or, in the case of the Bank of England, re-privatization), which needs to be replaced by the restoration of government oversight of central bank activities.

Much of the Post Keynesian critique of monetarism was soon confirmed, for example, by the experience of Thatcher's Britain, and some of it has been absorbed (without acknowledgement) into the New Neoclassical Synthesis (a horizontal LM curve, with the implication that interest rates are a more practical instrument of monetary policy than control of the money stock). But Post Keynesians remain severely critical of mainstream monetary policy, not least for its dogmatic assertion that output price inflation is the only legitimate target. This has led to a dangerous neglect of other important targets, most notably asset price inflation and the stability of the financial system as a whole (the vital question of "macroprudential regulation").

Post Keynesians also dispute the mainstream reliance on one single policy instrument: first, the stock of money, then – when this proved to be outside the control of the monetary authorities – the rate of interest. This renders the authorities powerless to influence the other target variables, a problem that is most obvious where asset price inflation is concerned. Housing and share price bubbles are recurrent and potentially very dangerous phenomena that might be deflated, or prevented altogether, by a sharp increase in interest rates at an early stage. But this may well have unacceptable consequences for output and employment, leaving the monetary authorities with no weapon at their disposal more powerful than verbal warnings to borrowers and (especially) to lenders, which in conditions of "irrational exuberance" may well be ignored.

While in the New Neoclassical Synthesis monetary policy operates only through changes in interest rates, which affect saving and (perhaps) business investment, Post Keynesians point to four additional channels, which are loosely related and in all likelihood more important (possibly much more important) than the interest rate channel. These are credit rationing in bad times and its opposite (credit abundance?) in good times; changes in asset prices, and in particular in expected asset prices, and the related phenomena of asset price bubbles and their sudden deflation; fear of default, which varies over time and may induce severe credit rationing at particular points in the cycle; and (related to this) the prospect of bankruptcy. The third and fourth factors are ruled out by the "no-Ponzi condition" imposed on the Dynamic Stochastic General Equilibrium (DSGE) models used by the mainstream. They introduce a crucial asymmetry in the wealth effects of monetary policy, as has often been noted since Irving Fisher developed his "debt deflation" theory of financial crisis.

There is general acceptance by Post Keynesians that one or more additional monetary policy instruments must be reinstated. Many favour a return to the use of direct controls, for example, to restrict mortgage lending when there are grounds to fear a housing price bubble or to increase margin requirements if share prices are being driven up by highly leveraged purchasers. Some argue for indirect controls that provide strong incentives for financial institutions to behave responsibly, for example, the imposition of asset-based reserve requirements that would in effect impose a higher tax on particular forms of lending to prevent the emergence of bubbles or to deflate them gradually (Palley 2004). There is also some controversy over the merits of monetary fine-tuning, with many Post Keynesians opposing frequent changes in interest rates and instead urging the maintenance of a stable – and very low – real interest rate. "Cheap money" has always been attractive on ethical grounds. Given that rentiers tend to be relatively well heeled, restricting their incomes by keeping interest rates very low will have desirable egalitarian consequences. It may also contribute to the maintenance of consumption and (especially) investment at levels consistent with full employment.

That said, Post Keynesians are also inclined to question how much monetary policy actually can achieve in a world of endogenous credit money. The failure of Quantitative Easing (QE) to stimulate a strong recovery in the United States and the United Kingdom in the wake of the Global Financial Crisis has not surprised them. Given the desire of the private sector to reduce its indebtedness by repaying loans and thereby reducing the demand for (and hence also the supply of) credit money, QE has not stimulated aggregate demand but has altered relative asset prices, allowing share prices and house values to increase but contributing relatively little to the real economy (Culham and King 2013). Like Keynes, who advocated the social control of investment to supplement the weak effects of expansionary monetary policy, Post Keynesians tend to focus on what monetary policy is unable to accomplish, and to advocate a set of more powerful alternatives. First and foremost, there is fiscal policy.

Fiscal policy

One significant difference between Old and New Keynesian economics is their treatment of fiscal policy. For Old Keynesians – and here they shared common ground with Post Keynesians – deficit-financed government expenditure was an important weapon against demand-deficient unemployment, while budget surpluses should be used to restrain demand-push inflation. New Classicals and many New Keynesians argue instead that fiscal policy is ineffective, invoking the principle of "Ricardian equivalence". Rational economic agents, it is claimed, will realize that increased government borrowing today entails higher taxation in the future and will reduce their consumption spending accordingly, eliminating any stimulatory effects of the increased government spending. Conversely, in the case of a budget surplus, government austerity measures will not reduce effective demand.

This principle was proclaimed two centuries ago by David Ricardo, and with some justification: in 1815 British government debt amounted to 300 per cent of GDP, annual interest payments represented approximately 10 per cent of national income, and there were real grounds for the wealthy to fear working-class resistance to any further increases in the taxation of necessities and to expect that any further government borrowing would therefore increase their own future tax bills. Even under these circumstances, Ricardo doubted the principle that is now associated with his name; even highly educated people, he believed, simply could not understand it. In this he was almost certainly correct.

A slightly different way in which the ineffectiveness of fiscal policy might be justified runs through monetary policy. If budget deficits place upward pressure on interest rates, thereby "crowding out" business investment, austerity measures may induce "crowding back in" and have no adverse effect on the level of effective demand. But this mechanism operates only if the loanable funds theory of interest is accepted. If the rate of interest is a purely monetary phenomenon, determined by the decisions of the monetary authorities, it will not be forced up by expansionary fiscal policy. If anything, the reverse is likely to occur, as higher government borrowing increases the balances held by the commercial banks with the central bank and reduces their need to borrow. Local authorities, state governments in federal systems and (of course) the individual nation-states that make up the eurozone can be constrained in their expenditure decisions by lack of finance. But there is no such "financial constraint" on government expenditure in an independent nation-state with its own sovereign currency (Hart 2011; Wray 2014).

There is some tension between Ricardian equivalence and the principle of "sound finance", as expressed in Angela Merkel's famous statement of "Swabian housewife logic": "every housewife knows that we cannot live beyond our means". In fact the two propositions are inconsistent: if fiscal policy is ineffective, then budget deficits cannot have *any* effects, adverse or otherwise. Post Keynesians, however, deny both the ineffec- tiveness of fiscal policy and the principle of sound finance enunciated by Merkel. Instead they assert the principle of "functional finance" that was first stated by Abba Lerner 70 years ago, in a short article and at greater length in his book on *The Economics of Control*: the only thing that matters in the operation of fiscal policy is the achievement of full employment and the avoidance of demand inflation (Lerner 1943, 1944, chapter 24; see also Burger 2003).

The principle of functional finance requires that the government should run a deficit if private sector expenditure is expected to be inadequate to maintain full employment, and it should run a surplus if private sector spending is expected to be excessive and thus to gen- erate demand inflation. A balanced budget is called for only in the exceptional case in which private sector spending is expected to be just right. Applying Merkel's logic in depressed conditions, when con- sumers lack confidence and business expectations are subdued, will be self-defeating: it will reduce effective demand, cut tax revenues and increase the budget deficit. This was one of the most important lessons of the Great Depression of the 1930s, which now needs to be learned all over again.

Thus Swabian housewife logic is fundamentally misconceived. The national debt is not a burden on posterity. It is not a burden on the nation, nor is it a sign of national poverty. The interest on the national debt is not a burden on the nation. The nation cannot be forced into bankruptcy. This is because neither the nation nor the government is an ordinary business concern (still less a Swabian housewife). In Lerner's words:

> The government, even if it does not want to raise the money by taxes, can always meet its obligations to any citizen by borrowing from another citizen or by printing the money to pay him. The nation cannot be thrown into a debtor's prison or debarred by a bankruptcy order from continuing its business. The weird notion of a country "going bankrupt" because it has a great internal debt can only be explained as the result of private capitalists building up a conception of the state in their own image and impressing this capitalist mythology on the other members of the capitalist society. (Lerner 1944, p. 304)

Lerner did acknowledge that serious problems may arise if the national debt is largely overseas-owned. He recognized two of these problems: the national government *can* be forced to repay (or else to choose the option of default), and interest payments *are* a loss to the nation. He did not discuss a third potential cause for concern: the possible exchange rate instability that may arise when foreign creditors react to increased, or decreased, confidence in the ability of the creditor country to service the debt. This is an empirical question, as is the possible negative effect on the growth rate of an unstable exchange rate. None of this entails that borrowing from foreigners is necessarily a bad idea. It "may be foolish or wise according to circumstances, just as in the case of individual borrowing" (p. 305). Where the government debt is largely or entirely owned by the nation's own citizens, however, none of these problems arises.

For Lerner, the principle of functional finance was a rather obvious corollary of the macroeconomics of the *General Theory*. Keynes, however, was reluctant to accept it, for reasons which remain rather obscure but which may reflect his doubts about its political acceptability (Aspromourgos 2014). It provides a very clear basis for criticizing the austerity measures adopted by the United Kingdom and by the eurozone countries in the aftermath of the Global Financial Crisis, as we shall see in the next chapter. But there is room for disagreement about the precise details of its implementation. As with monetary policy, there is some dispute among Post Keynesians concerning the merits of fiscal fine-tuning, which Hyman Minsky (for example) always opposed on the grounds that the time-lags involved in formulating and implementing policy changes were likely to produce unexpected and perverse results: fiscal stimulus when the economy was already recovering, or fiscal restraint after it had begun to turn down. Christopher Dow (1964) provides a classic account of these forecasting errors and their consequences in the United Kingdom between 1945 and 1960.

Note that this is not an argument for reducing the size of the state. In fact Minsky was a "Big Government" man, for two reasons. The "flow" argument for a high ratio of government spending to GDP is that built-in fiscal stabilizers are much more powerful when G/Y is 30 per cent or more (as in the United States after 1945) than when it was little more than 10 per cent (in 1929, at the start of the Great Depression). The "stock" argument concerns the effects of all past deficits, which have generated a huge quantity of risk-free government liabilities that appear in the balance sheets of private sector financial institutions as risk-free assets, and had thus contributed to the greatly reduced financial fragility of the post-1945 US economy compared with the situation in 1929 (Minsky 1982). There is a more general lesson to be learned from this: the need for stock-flow consistent modelling, as advocated by Wynne Godley and Marc Lavoie (2007).

Prices and incomes policy

Contractionary fiscal policy is an appropriate weapon against demand inflation, but as Sidney Weintraub argued half a century ago, it is likely to be both ineffective and damaging when applied to cost inflation. In this case direct intervention in product and factor markets is required. In the highly unionized labour markets of the post-1945 "golden age", the most important principle was to ensure that money wages did not rise too rapidly. As early as 1951 Nicholas Kaldor had established the underlying principle, in a paper that was for some reason not published at the time. Assuming that the existing distribution of total output between capital and labour is acceptable, money wages in all industries should increase at the same annual rate as labour productivity. Industries with below-average productivity growth should be allowed to raise their prices, and industries where productivity was growing faster should be required to reduce prices, so that the overall price level remains roughly constant.

Kaldor did not support above-average pay increases for workers in industries (or individual companies) with above-average productivity growth. This, he noted, entailed below-average increases for other workers, who would, in effect, be subsidizing their inefficient employers. Thus he was not sympathetic to the practice of "productivity bargaining" at the industry or company level ("enterprise bargaining", as it came to be known in Australia). In a small open economy the Kaldor rule needs to be modified to allow for variations in the terms of trade, which change the effective rate of productivity growth. Thus improvements in the terms of trade allow slightly higher wage increases, and conversely when the terms of trade deteriorate (Kaldor 1964).

A prices and incomes policy of this type can be implemented in several ways: by legally binding compulsory arbitration, as in Australia before 1990; by agreement between the "social partners", as in the formerly social democratic or "corporatist" countries of Northern Europe; or through the use of tax incentives and disincentives, as proposed by Wallich and Weintraub (1971) for the United States (but never implemented, there or elsewhere). Under this last proposal, for a "Tax-based Incomes Policy" (or TIP), companies would be free to pay wage increases that exceeded the norm, but they would face a progressively increasing tax bill on the excess, and this would provide a clear financial incentive for wage moderation.

Some Post Keynesians advocate an alternative way of restraining wage inflation. If the state were to act as employer of last resort, Hyman Minsky suggested, offering a job at a low but socially acceptable wage to all those unable to find better-paid employment in the private sector, this would not only eliminate demand-deficient unemployment but would also control wage inflation. Excessive wage demand by unions would be constrained by their members' fear that well-paid jobs in the private sector would be replaced by low-wage employment in the public sector (Minsky 2008, pp. 310–13). This proposal, derived from the Works Progress Administration under the New Deal, has attracted some support (Tcherneva 2012; Wray 1998). Other Post Keynesians criticize it as a punitive measure that resembles the unacceptable "work for the dole" requirements imposed by conservative governments in the age of neoliberalism, and doubt its ability to deliver either full employment or price stability (Sawyer 2003).

Incomes policies of all types broke down during the stagflationary crisis of the 1970s, in part under the pressure of rapidly rising primary product prices (which pose quite different problems, and will be discussed in the following section). Since then trade unions have been very substantially weakened in almost all parts of the advanced capitalist world, and the threat of renewed wage-push inflation now seems rather remote. Today a rather different case can be made for an incomes policy, this time to avoid the dangers of deflation and a continually declining share of wages. Instead of restraining real wages, an incomes policy now needs to make sure that they rise in line with labour productivity, so that unit labour costs do not fall. By July 2014 even the doggedly anti-inflationary Bundesbank was calling for real wages in Germany to increase, after a decade and a half of stagnation (Hermann 2014). It was time, the German monetary authorities now believed, for the share of profits in GDP to stop rising. Whether any of this can be achieved in a neoliberal world in which unions have been greatly weakened, labour markets are subject to continuing deregulation (actually re-regulation in the interests of capital) and important nations like Germany do not even (as of December 2014) have a statutory minimum wage is not at all clear.

Two important broader issues are involved here. The first concerns the inter-disciplinary nature of the problem: macroeconomic issues cannot be understood in isolation from the political and social system in which the economy is embedded and from the prevailing ideological orthodoxy. Post Keynesians have a much better grasp of these inter-dependencies than the great majority of mainstream economists, but they do need to be kept constantly in mind.

The second issue is more narrowly economic. Post Keynesians working in the Kaleckian tradition have drawn a distinction between "wage-led" and "profit-led" regimes, and this has profound implications for wages policy. A decline in the share of wages will reduce consumption expenditure, but it will also tend to increase investment spending (by raising profits) and net exports (through the reduction in domestic costs and hence in the relative prices of exports and imports). If the negative effect on consumption is greater than the positive effect on investment and net exports, we are dealing with a wage-led regime, and conversely for a profit-led regime. The evidence suggests that for most rich countries domestic demand is wage-led, but that in many cases the net export effect is strong enough to produce a profit-led regime overall, when both domestic and foreign demand are considered together.

It is important to avoid a rather obvious fallacy of composition here: not all countries can increase their net exports, so that for Planet Earth as a whole a wage-led regime is much more likely than it is for any individual nation-state. Wage-led deflation, like that forced through in Germany in the early years of the new millennium by means of severe cuts to welfare payments for the unemployed (the notorious Hartz IV programme), is a "beggar-thy-neighbour" policy similar to the competitive devaluations that did so much damage in the 1930s. The latest estimates suggest that a uniform global one percentage point reduction in the wage share would reduce global GDP by 0.36 percentage points (Stockhammer and Onaran 2013, p. 70). I shall return to this question in the following chapter.

International economic policy

The need for international coordination of macroeconomic policy is especially obvious in the context of wages policy, but it is by no means confined to questions of labour costs and income distribution. In the "golden age" of advanced capitalism from 1945 to 1973 unemployment and inflation were very low, output grew rapidly and downturns in economic activity were brief and insubstantial. To some extent this was the result of the international economic order that had been decided upon at the Bretton Woods conference in 1944, where Keynes succeeded in implementing part (but only part) of his ambitious agenda for postwar financial reconstruction. A fixed exchange rate regime restored stability and eliminated the self-defeating competitive currency devaluations of the 1930s, while controls over capital movements prevented any repetition of the destabilizing "hot money" flows of that decade. Trade grew rapidly in the 1950s and 1960s, but international finance was deliberately repressed. The Bretton Woods era ended in 1973 with the devaluation of the US dollar, the consequent return to floating exchange rates and the liberalization of global capital flows. Many Post Keynesians attribute the less favourable macroeconomic performance of the last 40 years in some part to the breakdown of the Bretton Woods system.

There is, however, some disagreement as to how the international monetary system might be reformed. There is broad agreement on the underlying principles, which include a substantial degree of re-regulation of global financial markets; prevention of neo-mercantilist strategies like the deflationary wage policies that were criticized in the previous section; and acceptance that responsibility for correcting global imbalances should be shared by surplus and deficit countries, by creditors and debtors, as Keynes had unsuccessfully urged in 1944 at Bretton Woods, rather than imposed on deficit countries alone.

As always, the devil is in the detail. The most ambitious proposal for the reform of the international monetary system comes from Paul Davidson, who urges the adoption of Keynes's plan for an International Clearing Union (ICU). This would not only re-establish fixed exchange rates but would also require all international payments to be made by governments, through the ICU. This would eliminate private sector transactions in foreign exchange altogether, and would thereby involve a massive reduction in both the volume and the influence of global finance (Davidson 2009).

This is too radical for many Post Keynesians. In particular, advocates of "modern monetary theory" like Randall Wray oppose any return to fixed exchange rates on the grounds that this would entail an unacceptable loss of national sovereignty (Wray 2006). Other Post Keynesians object that leaving the value of one's currency to the vagaries of speculative global currency markets implies a rather strange interpretation of "sovereignty", but the supporters of floating exchange rates do have a point. The well-known "trifecta theorem" tells us that a national government cannot opt for fixed exchange rates, free capital movements *and* an independent monetary policy: it can choose any two of these, but not all three. In response to this trilemma many Post Keynesians advocate capital controls, not floating exchange rates.

There is more general support for the reform of the International Monetary Fund to make it the world central bank that Keynes had envisaged, well resourced and with a commitment to promoting full employment on a global scale. Similarly, there is a strong case for removing the residual traces of the "Washington Consensus" from the World Bank and converting it into an agency that will promote the development of the poorest countries on the basis of the analysis of economic development that was outlined in the previous chapter (D'Arista and Erturk 2013). Most Post Keynesians also advocate the introduction of a turnover tax on international financial transactions (the so-called Tobin tax) to raise revenue and perhaps also put "sand in the wheels" of speculative international finance (Grahl and Lysandrou 2003). Again, international agreement would be needed, and the benefits would include a reduction in the volatility of exchange markets.

In recent years the financialization of primary product markets has greatly increased the speculative influences on the determination of commodity prices at the expense of the more fundamental forces of product supply and demand. The consequent increase in the instability in food and raw material prices has revived interest in the proposal made by Kaldor and Jan Tinbergen back in the 1960s for the establishment of a set of international funds to intervene in primary product markets in order to stabilize commodity prices (Ussher 2009). This would remove one major source of cost inflation, and it would also allow the general introduction of the principles of "fair trade", to the benefit of poor people in primary producing countries.

Environmental policy

On the many issues surrounding environmental policy at the micro-economic level, Post Keynesians have a distinctive and important contribution to make, despite their relatively sparse contribution in this area to date. This stems from the very limited role that they place on substitution effects, in both production and consumption, and, related to this, their doubts concerning the role of prices in an economy dominated by large corporations with oligopolistic market power. Thus the market cannot be relied upon to provide reliable indices either of the Marginal Social Damage (MSD) of pollution or of the Marginal Abatement Cost (MAC). It is unlikely that pollution taxes will be sufficient to bring MSD into equality with MAC, so that there is a strong case for direct government intervention to supplement the price mechanism. Post Keynesians advocate a number of forms of direct action, including setting minimum environmental standards and renewable energy targets, measures to change consumer tastes and habits, and a public investment policy to promote innovation and overcome the constraints on green investment that may be imposed by credit rationing by lenders and fundamental uncertainty on the part of potential borrowers (Holt et al. 2009; Perry 2013).

These microeconomic proposals serve to differentiate Post Keynesian thinking on environmental policy from that of the mainstream. But there is an additional very large and irreducibly macroeconomic dimension to the problem. If, to prevent dangerous and irreversible environmental damage from global warming, it is necessary to cut aggregate consumption, or at the very least to reduce the rate of growth of consumption, how can this be achieved without initiating a serious recession? This is not a problem for mainstream macroeconomics, since even if reduced consumption were somehow to occur unexpectedly (as a "shock"), it would induce appropriate equilibrium responses from economic agents, including an increase in leisure time but no rise in (involuntary) unemployment. Post Keynesians, however, share the concerns of the man and woman in the street, who do not believe that the world operates like this. Thus they advocate substantial increases in environmentally friendly public investment in order to maintain effective demand and prevent a sharp increase in involuntary unemployment. The move to an ecologically sustainable global economy requires growth that is "slower by design, not disaster", to quote the sub-title of an influential book by Peter Victor (2008).

The details of a distinctively Post Keynesian environmental macroeconomics are still being worked out (Fontana and Sawyer 2013). Its implementation will almost certainly require a substantial degree of international cooperation, for at least two closely related reasons. First, the balance of payments constraints considered in Chapter 6 might otherwise constrain an individual nation's ability to engage in "green investment" on the appropriate scale. Second, the Verdoorn relationship between output growth and productivity growth suggests that any nation that opts for a faster deceleration of output growth than its competitors may suffer additional costs in the form of reduced international competitiveness. If these problems can be resolved, the macroeconomic effects of massive green investment expenditure will be equally large, and there will be very beneficial consequences for employment (Pollin et al. 2014, chapters 6–7).

References

Arestis, P. 2013. "Economic theory and policy: a coherent post-Keynesian approach", *European Journal of Economics and Economic Policies: Intervention*, 10(2), 243–55.

Aspromourgos, T. 2014. "Keynes, Lerner, and the question of public debt", *History of Political Economy*, 46(3), Fall, 409–33.

Balogh, T. 1982. *The Irrelevance of Conventional Economics*, London: Weidenfeld & Nicolson.

Burger, P. 2003. *Sustainable Fiscal Policy and Economic Stability: Theory and Practice*, Cheltenham, UK and Northampton, MA, USA: Edward Elgar.

Culham, J. and J.E. King. 2013. "*Horizontalists and Verticalists* after 25 years", *Review of Keynesian Economics*, 1(4), 391–405.

D'Arista, J. and K. Erturk. 2013. "Global imbalances and the international monetary system: problems and proposals", in M.H. Wolfson and G.A. Epstein (eds), *The Handbook of the Political Economy of Financial Crises*, Oxford: Oxford University Press, pp. 230–47.

Davidson, P. 2009. *The Keynes Solution: The Path to Global Economic Prosperity*, Basingstoke: Palgrave Macmillan.

Dow, J.C.R. 1964. *The Management of the British Economy 1945–60*, Cambridge: Cambridge University Press.

Fontana, G. and M. Sawyer. 2013. "Post-Keynesian and Kaleckian thoughts on ecological macroeconomics", *European Journal of Economics and Economic Policies: Intervention*, **10**(2), 256–67.

Godley, W. and M. Lavoie. 2007. *Monetary Economics: An Integrated Approach to Credit, Money, Income, Production and Wealth*, Basingstoke: Palgrave Macmillan.

Grahl, J. and P. Lysandrou. 2003. "Sand in the wheels or spanner in the works? The Tobin tax and global finance", *Cambridge Journal of Economics*, **27**(4), July, 597–621.

Hart, N. 2011. "Macroeconomic policy and Abba Lerner's system of functional finance", *Economic Papers*, **30**(2), June, 208–17.

Hermann, U. 2014. "Bundesbank: Löhne müssen steigen!" ("Bundesbank: real wages must rise"), *Die Tageszeitung* (Berlin), 22 July, p. 5.

Holt, R.P.F., S. Pressman and C. Spash (eds). 2009. *Post Keynesian and Ecological Economics: Confronting Environmental Issues*, Cheltenham, UK and Northampton, MA, USA: Edward Elgar.

Kaldor, N. 1964. "Prospects of a wages policy for Australia", *Economic Record*, **40**(90), June, 145–55.

Kaldor, N. 1982. *The Scourge of Monetarism*, Oxford: Oxford University Press.

Keynes, J.M. 1936. *The General Theory of Employment, Interest and Money*, London: Macmillan.

Lerner, A.P. 1943. "Functional finance and the federal debt", *Social Research*, **10**(1), February, 38–51.

Lerner, A.P. 1944. *The Economics of Control: Principles of Welfare Economics*, New York: Macmillan.

Minsky, H.P. 1982. *Can "It" Happen Again? Essays on Instability and Finance*, Armonk, NY: M.E. Sharpe.

Minsky, H.P. 2008. *Stabilizing an Unstable Economy*, second edn, New York: McGraw-Hill.

Palley, T. 2004. "Asset based reserve requirements: reasserting domestic monetary control in an era of financial innovation and instability", *Review of Political Economy*, **16**(1), January, 43–53.

Perry, N. 2013. "Environmental economics and policy", in G.C. Harcourt and P. Kriesler (eds), *The Oxford Handbook of Post-Keynesian Economics, Volume 2: Critiques and Methodology*, Oxford: Oxford University Press, pp. 391–411.

Pigou, A.C. 1937. *Socialism versus Capitalism*, London: Macmillan.

Pixley, J., S. Whimster and S. Wilson. 2013. "Central bank independence: a social economic and democratic critique", *Economic and Labour Relations Review*, **24**(1), March, 32–50.

Pollin, R., H. Garrett-Peltier, J. Heintz and B. Hendricks. 2014. *Green Growth: A U.S. Program for Controlling Climate Change and Expanding Employment Opportunities*, Amherst, MA: Center for American Progress.

Pressman, S. 2014. "Keynes, family allowances, and Keynesian economic policy", *Review of Keynesian Economics*, **2**(4), 508–26.

Sawyer, M.C. 2003. "Employer of last resort: could it deliver full employment and price stability?" *Journal of Economic Issues*, **37**(4), December, 881–907.

Skidelsky, R. 2009. *Keynes: The Return of the Master*, London: Allen Lane.

Stockhammer, E. and O. Onaran. 2013. "Wage-led growth: theory, evidence, policy", *Review of Keynesian Economics*, **1**(4), Winter, 61–78.

Tcherneva, P.R. 2012. "Permanent on-the-spot job creation – the missing Keynes plan for full employment and economic transformation", *Review of Social Economy*, **70**(1), March, 57–80.

Tinbergen, J. 1956. *Economic Policy: Principles and Design*, Amsterdam: North-Holland.

Ussher, L.J. 2009. "Global imbalances and the key currency regime: the case for a commodity reserve currency", *Review of Political Economy*, **21**(3), July, 403–21.

Victor, P.A. 2008. *Managing Without Growth: Slower by Design, Not Disaster*, Cheltenham, UK and Northampton, MA, USA: Edward Elgar.

Wallich, H.C. and E.R. Weintraub. 1971. "A tax-based incomes policy", *Journal of Economic Issues*, **5**(2), June, 1–19.

Wray, L.R. 1998. *Understanding Modern Money: The Key to Full Employment and Price Stability*, Cheltenham, UK and Lyme, NH, USA: Edward Elgar.

Wray, L.R. 2006. "To fix or float: theoretical and pragmatic considerations", in L.-P. Rochon and S. Rossi (eds), *Monetary and Exchange Rate Systems: A Global View of Financial Crises*, Cheltenham, UK and Northampton, MA, USA: Edward Elgar, pp. 210–31.

Wray, L.R. 2014. "From the state theory of money to modern money theory: an alternative to economic orthodoxy", Working Paper No. 792, Levy Economics Institute of Bard College, Annandale-on-Hudson, NY.

8 A case study: the Global Financial Crisis

Minsky revisited

Although few Post Keynesians can claim to have foreseen the Global Financial Crisis (GFC), in the sense that they predicted the precise timing or the specific details of the events of 2007–08, they were not at all surprised by it, since it was entirely consistent with their long-standing critique of neoliberal, global financial capitalism (Hein 2012). As we have seen in previous chapters, Post Keynesians insist that money is not neutral, the classical dichotomy is a fallacy, and the New Classical/New Neoclassical Synthesis emphasis on "real business cycles" diverts theoretical attention from the crucial interactions between money and finance, on the one hand, and output and employment, on the other.

Hyman Minsky's work on financial fragility is fundamental to an understanding of the GFC (King 2010). Minsky stressed both the cyclical instability of finance-dominated capitalism and the role of financial innovation (and hence of institutional and structural change). In a world characterized by fundamental uncertainty concerning future prospects, rather than by quantifiable risk, the expectations of lenders and borrowers fluctuate (often dramatically) in a regularly repeated cyclical process. Depression gives way to confidence, which grows into exuberance and excitement before collapsing into despair. These mood swings are reflected in financial transactions, as caution is replaced first by optimism and then by euphoria.

For Minsky, neither consumption nor investment is particularly interest-elastic, and the effects of changes in interest rates are in any case often swamped by other factors. He distinguishes three ways in which financial events have important effects on the real economy. First and foremost, changes in asset prices lead to changes in both consumption and investment spending. Two different mechanisms operate here. Consumption depends on wealth as well as income, so that increases in the price of land and financial securities induce agents to increase their consumption expenditure, and vice versa. Investment depends (inter alia) on the relative price of existing assets and newly produced capital goods. When asset prices collapse, due to the "fire sales" required to meet financial commitments, the incentive to buy new capital goods falls; the reverse is true (more weakly, perhaps) when asset prices are rising.

The second way in which financial conditions affect aggregate expenditure, and therefore output and employment, is through changes in expectations. Minsky was not a believer in rational expectations. Indeed, the financial instability hypothesis can be summarized as a theory of cyclically irrational expectations, as speculative finance gives way to Ponzi finance and then, after the credit crunch, to hedge finance once more. Note that it is expectations concerning asset prices that really matter; "inflationary expectations" as conventionally defined, which are about the future rate of increase of output prices, are much less important.

The third channel through which finance affects output and employment is critical in the crisis and depression phases of the cycle. This is credit rationing. Whereas in the upswing and (especially) the euphoric phase almost everyone capable of asking for a loan is granted one, when the bubble bursts even solid, creditworthy borrowers will be denied finance, and will be forced to reduce their expenditure accordingly. Minsky himself emphasized the power of credit rationing in reducing business investment in the depression phase of the cycle, but he would not have been greatly surprised to discover that it also had an adverse effect on consumer expenditure, including (but not confined to) housing. Again, this has little or nothing to do with interest rates. In a credit crunch, almost by definition, it is impossible to obtain finance at any price.

Minsky believed that the Federal Reserve had learned the lessons of 1929, and this had contributed greatly to the increased stability of the US economy after 1945. Although financial instability could never be prevented it could be managed, as indeed it had been in a number of postwar crises, like those of 1966 and 1987 (on which see Minsky 1988). The GFC of 2007–08 was not, of course, a simple re-run of the financial crises of the past, and Minsky would not have expected it to be so. The central dynamic of the financial instability hypothesis is provided by financial innovation: new lenders, new borrowers, new products and new ways of avoiding regulation. Minsky himself saw the importance of securitization (Minsky 1987), and began to think about a new stage in the development of the financial sector, which he termed "money manager capitalism" (Wray 2009), in which new financial instruments were created, and new financial institutions were continually eroding the banks' share of assets and liabilities, forcing them into more and more risky forms of behaviour.

He might well have been surprised by the magnitude of the US housing bubble in the early years of the twenty-first century, and perhaps also by the role of household debt, relative to corporate debt, in the unfolding of the crisis. But he would not have been at all surprised by the rise of "shadow banking", nor by the ability of these new financial institutions to escape effective regulation (Gabor 2014). In broad terms, though, Minsky's "Wall Street vision" of the capitalist system was dramatically vindicated by the GFC, and his financial instability hypothesis is an essential part of the explanation of it.

Financialization in practice and theory

Post Keynesians use the term "financialization" to summarize the historical process that began in the late 1960s, towards the end of the postwar "golden age", and culminated half a century later in the GFC (Hein and van Treeck 2010). In practice, financialization involved the emergence of new "products" (new assets and liabilities), new suppliers and new customers. It had a quantitative dimension, with a sharp rise in the proportion of GDP, employment and (especially) corporate profits accounted for by the FIRE sector (finance, insurance and real estate). There was also a qualitative dimension, with a very significant increase in the economic and political power of finance. This is often described as representing an epochal shift from one stage of capitalism to another: from the manufacturing-based "Fordist" era of the "golden age" to a new era of "finance-led growth" (or Minsky's "money manager capitalism").

There was a third dimension to the process of financialization: the increased cultural and symbolic power of finance. This is related to the Marxian themes of alienation (in which people are controlled by their own products, whether they realize it or not) and fetishism (in which they falsely attribute human powers to these products). Under capitalism, for example, workers are dominated by the machines that they themselves have made, and sometimes see these machines as being the source of their employers' profits, rather than their own surplus labour. When finance becomes the end of all economic activity, and the production of useful goods and services becomes the means, we are all in the grip of a sort of second-order alienation and fetishism, which is difficult to recognize and even more difficult to overcome. Even the most perceptive heterodox economists have neglected this question, which is, however, brilliantly dissected by the anthropologists Edward LiPuma and Benjamin Lee. Any programme of definancialization will need to overcome the culture of finance, "a power that seems answerable to no other power" (LiPuma and Lee 2004, p. 189).

All this was made possible by the thorough-going deregulation of finance that began with the collapse of Bretton Woods and will be dissected in the following section. This process of deregulation was in turn encouraged by neoliberal ideology. Four principles of neoliberal economics were directly relevant here. First, there was the case for floating exchange rates made by the monetarists. Second, there was the new financial economics, including the Capital Asset Pricing Model and in particular the "efficient markets hypothesis", according to which markets always make the best possible use of all available information, so that detailed regulation is unnecessary (since "the price is right"). Third, New Classical macroeconomics revived Say's Law and the doctrine of the neutrality of money, repudiating the principle of effective demand. Finally, there was the deeply held belief that market failure was almost always less serious than state failure, which undermined the case for any form of regulation, micro or macro.

The efficient markets hypothesis was especially important. It purported to apply the New Classical principle of rational expectations to financial transactions, the inference being that financial markets invariably produce the "right price" and therefore require only the lightest of government regulation. This inference involves the elementary logical error of affirming the consequent. The truth of "If A then B" does not entail the truth of "If B then A". Here A is efficiency of financial markets and B is the inability of market participants to outperform the market for any length of time. The fallacy was recognized by some perceptive critics before the onset of the GFC, who noted that the propositions that "prices are right" and that "there is no free lunch" are not equivalent statements. While both statements are true in an efficient market, "no free lunch" can also be true in an inefficient market. Even if prices are not at their fundamental values, this does not entail that there are any excess profits for the taking (Barberis and Thaler 2003, p. 1057).

A similar criticism was made by the former head of the (British) Financial Services Authority, Adair Turner (2009, pp. 39–42), and by the Old Keynesian James Tobin, who distinguished four quite distinct meanings of "efficiency" in financial markets. The first, "information arbitrage efficiency", or "technical efficiency", was equivalent to the "no free lunch" position. Tobin was very clear that efficiency in his second sense, "fundamental valuation efficiency", was not entailed by technical efficiency, since the market moves up and down much more than can be justified by changes in rationally formed expectations. His third meaning was "full insurance efficiency", allowing economic agents to protect themselves against all possible future contingencies. There had been a proliferation of new financial markets and instruments in the 1970s and early 1980s, the contribution of which to market efficiency he regarded with scepticism. The fourth meaning, "fundamental efficiency", referred to the services that the FIRE sector performs for the economy as a whole, and on this matter, too, Tobin was highly critical. His conclusion, in a public lecture delivered as long ago as 1984, resonates powerfully in the wake of the GFC. Far too many resources were being thrown into financial activities that were remote from the production of goods and services, generating high private rewards disproportionate to their benefits to society (Tobin 1987).

In the decade or so leading up to the GFC the efficient markets hypothesis did a great deal of harm, both in encouraging foolhardy behaviour on a massive scale by large corporate players in financial markets and in discouraging any serious attempt at regulating their activities. Outside the FIRE sector, the consequences of financialization were no less profound. Most important was the return of "shareholder value" as the only viable goal of the capitalist corporation. During the "golden age", alternatives to (short-run) profit maximization were accepted, like the "stakeholder capitalism" practised to some extent in Austria, Germany and Japan, where management, workers and local and national communities were considered to have a legitimate interest in the way the firm was run, along with the shareholders, and were encouraged to take a long-term view of these interests. At least in Northern Europe this was linked to the power of organized labour and to corporatist wage policies, and both here and in Japan income differentials were restrained. With the rise of shareholder value, the new rule for corporate behaviour is "distribute and downsize" rather than "reinvest and grow", and this has significant implications for Post Keynesian pricing theory (Dallery 2009). New incentive systems have been introduced, with bonuses for senior management tied to the company's share price, and this corresponds to a new alliance between management and shareholders at the expense of the old alliance between management and other stakeholders (Lazonick 2013).

All this has led to rapidly increasing inequality. Profits rose relative to wages, so that the share of wages in national income has steadily declined; top managerial salaries grew much more rapidly than the pay of their subordinates; and there has also been substantially increased inequality in wealth, stimulated by the rise in equity prices. Increasing inequality also encouraged the growth of debt. In part this was the inevitable result of financialization, since the rising sum of assets was necessarily accompanied by an increase in liabilities. To some extent it was a direct result of the increased inequality, with those left behind increasingly tempted – and increasingly able – to borrow in order to maintain their standard of living, purchase a house and protect their social status. In turn this was linked to a profound cultural shift, with the growing acceptance of a "debt culture" among rich and poor alike. Note the important and potentially sinister asymmetry that is involved with the growth of debt: debtors can be forced to cut their spending, but creditors cannot be forced to increase their expenditure when macroeconomic conditions deteriorate. The growth of consumer debt (especially housing debt) in the United States was a major contributor to the financial crisis of 2007–08 (Barba and Pivetti 2009; Kapeller and Schütz 2014).

This suggests a distinction between two very different macroeconomic regimes (Stockhammer 2013). In the "debt-led" or "finance-dominated" accumulation regime, consumption spending financed by credit grows strongly, through positive wealth effects on the consumption of the rich and through increasing debt that allows the consumption of the poor to continue to rise, even though their incomes do not. This regime characterized the Anglo-Saxon countries in the decade or so before the GFC. In the "export-driven" growth model exemplified by Germany and China, demand from overseas is much more important than domestic demand, and consumer debt increases much less rapidly. Both growth models suffer from a structural deficiency in demand, due to wage suppression. In the "debt-burdened" regime, financial instability comes to threaten both consumption and investment spending. In this model the growth of debt, and with it the emergence of financial fragility, is traced back to the real economy, and in particular to the institutional and political processes that have redistributed income away from workers to owners and top management. Stockhammer concludes that the GFC cannot be understood without a clear focus on the power relations between capital and labour.

The Global Financial Crisis: "made in America"

The GFC was the result of a toxic mix of globalization, financialization, deregulation, increasing inequality and rising debt, all encouraged (if not initiated) by the neoliberal ideas of mainstream macroeconomists. Globalization greatly increased the power of internationally footloose capital relative both to labour and national governments (Davidson 2002). By the early 1980s it was possible for "the markets" to punish social democratic governments in a way that would have been inconceivable 30 years earlier; the experience of the Mitterand government in France is a celebrated case in point. Remember that "the markets" are not a force of nature; they are social institutions that are operated by rich people, and the poor people who work for them.

The GFC of 2007–08 was "made in the USA" (just like the Great Depression of 1929–33), and transmitted internationally via trade, capital flows and (especially) expectations (again as in 1929–33, but this time much more quickly, due to the revolution in information technology). Some prominent mainstream economists attributed the GFC to the deep cuts in US interest rates imposed by the Federal Reserve in the early years of the new century. This is profoundly unconvincing as an explanation of the GFC, but it is a reasonable inference from the New Neoclassical Synthesis, according to which the only monetary transmission channel is the rate of interest. So long as the monetary authorities get interest rates right, there is no prospect that financial instability can lead to instability in the real economy. Thus turbulence in financial markets can have no significant real economic consequences unless it is the result of serious monetary policy errors.

In fact, as we have seen, the underlying cause of the GFC was financial fragility, made much worse by deregulation. The proximate cause was the bursting of the US housing bubble, which led to a fall in consumption spending (through negative wealth effects), the collapse of housing investment and the eventual fall in financial derivative values that led to the failure of Lehman Brothers in September 2008. Thus any comprehensive and convincing explanation of the GFC would have to go far beyond the impact of lower interest rates on US house prices to consider the increasing financialization of the US (and the global) economy; the dismantling of much of the New Deal system of financial regulation, and the systematic evasion of those regulations that remained; the rise of a free market fundamentalism that cast doubt on the need for anything more than self-regulation of supposedly "efficient" financial markets governed by "rational expectations"; the lag of real wages behind the growth in labour productivity, so that workers' consumption was increasingly funded by debt; and the continuing attrition of trade union power and effective government regulation of the labour market, which allowed this to happen – the whole fabric of neoliberalism, in effect.

There is some dispute over whether the GFC really was a "Minsky moment", as it has often been described. Paul Davidson denies this, on the grounds that the so-called NINJA mortgagees ("no income, no jobs, no assets") were not Ponzi borrowers in Minsky's sense. The GFC, he argues, should instead be viewed in a more general sense as a crisis of de-leveraging (Davidson 2008). The Minskyans respond by pointing to the role of financial innovation, the new stage of money manager capitalism, the deregulation and the evasion of remaining controls over financial markets, and the increasing loss of memory of lenders in the period immediately before 2007, all of which they claim to be entirely consistent with the underlying principles of the financial fragility hypothesis.

There is, however, no disagreement about the fundamental role played by the deregulation of financial markets in the decades leading up to the GFC. It all began in the international currency markets after the collapse of the Bretton Woods system in the early 1970s. In the United States, the weakening or elimination of regulation soon spread to the equity and housing markets, with the destruction of the New Deal housing finance system giving rise first to the Savings and Loan crisis of the 1980s and then to the perilous innovation of mortgage securitization. By the late 1990s the repeal of the Glass-Steagall Act separating retail banking from more speculative financial activities had produced the phenomenon of regulatory holes, or true shadow markets, in which financial activity escaped oversight entirely (Silver 2013). Pressure from the industry meant that the financial derivatives market soon became entirely unregulated, while decisions by both Congress and the Supreme Court greatly weakened the rights of investors to take action against underwriters, lawyers and accountants. Mortgage brokers were lightly supervised, and the subsidiaries of commercial banks and building societies, which accounted for 30 per cent of sub-prime loans, were less closely supervised than their parent companies. The Federal Reserve refused to define acceptable rules for non-prime lending and failed to prevent the rapid growth of bank holding company leverage in the run-up to the crisis. No regulator had responsibility for overseeing the asset-backed commercial paper market (Jarsulic 2013).

Deregulation in the global economy compounded all these problems. As Martin Wolfson notes, there is a strong element of cumulative causation in this process of financialization, since the greater power of financial institutions makes effective regulation less likely, further increasing the influence of finance (Wolfson 2013). It is important also to recognize that "regulatory capture" applies to macroeconomic policy institutions no less than to their microeconomic counterparts: to central banks as well as to industry regulators. Thomas Palley emphasizes the need for central banks to be more intellectually open-minded and to recognize the dangers of "cognitive capture" by the financial markets. He is especially critical of the way in which the Federal Reserve is protected by its patronage of academic economists, which includes a revolving door with university economics departments, providing the Federal Reserve with intellectual cover and legitimacy that it might otherwise not enjoy (Palley 2013).

What have we learned? I: economists against austerity

In the aftermath of the GFC, a group of British economists established a network that they called Economists Against Austerity (see https://economistsagainstausterity.wordpress.com). They argued that the Post Keynesian principle of functional finance was especially relevant in the period of sustained economic downturn that began in 2008 and came to be known as the Great Recession, and it required a cyclical increase in government spending, not cuts. The initial reaction to the GFC of several Western governments was consistent with this principle. In the United States, Britain, France and Australia, the Bush/Obama, Brown, Sarkozy and Rudd administrations responded with packages of bail-outs, cheap money and fiscal stimulus. "We are all Keynesians now", they might have claimed, even though their economic advisers were not Post Keynesians but instead adhered to the New Neoclassical Synthesis and would have found it difficult to reconcile their support for the package with their position on matters of macroeconomic theory.

The bail-outs and bank deposit guarantees were probably inevitable, and they were certainly very welcome. Almost anything would have been better than a repetition of the chain of bank failures in the early 1930s that undoubtedly deepened and lengthened the Great Depression. Whatever the nature of the monetary transmission mechanism, there would have been serious consequences if any financial institution had been allowed to go under after the collapse of Lehman Brothers. It is possible to argue over the details. The bail-outs certainly could and should have been designed in such a way as to punish severely the shareholders and senior managers of the institutions that were rescued, while protecting depositors, employees and (so far as possible) the taxpayer. This would have been desirable both on equity grounds and to reduce the moral hazard implications. In this regard the virtual nationalization of several banks by the British government was preferable to the open-ended commitments made to private financial institutions by the US and Australian administrations.

The return of cheap money was also welcome. Although in a deep recession the use of monetary policy may indeed be like "pushing on a string" (as Keynes is supposed to have said), the alternative was certainly worse. Post Keynesian commentators interpreted the drastic reductions in interest rates in all the advanced capitalist economies as a de facto abandonment of inflation targeting in favour of employment targeting (Arestis and Sawyer 2008). The third and most important part of the package was a substantial fiscal stimulus, entirely consistent with the Post Keynesian model of an economy threatened by collapsing aggregate demand but very difficult to square with the implications of the New Neoclassical Synthesis. Again, it was possible to object to some of the details. A fiscal stimulus can be designed to be more or less egalitarian. There was a very strong case for making direct cash payments to the poor, instead of providing tax relief for the rich. In Australia the Rudd government's December 2008 and February 2009 "bonus" payments to low- and middle-income employees, farmers, aged pensioners, disabled people and carers was a step in the right direction, but these payments were notoriously withheld from the unemployed in what seemed to be an unacknowledged act of discrimination between the "deserving" and the "undeserving" poor.

But the pressure for austerity measures has been unrelenting, above all in the eurozone, where the "Swabian housewife logic" that was criticized in the previous chapter has been very influential. In reaction, a sort of Kalecki–Minsky synthesis has been developed by Richard Koo, who draws on the Japanese experience since 1990 to illustrate the dangers of a severe "balance sheet recession", in which an over-indebted private sector cuts consumption and investment expenditure in order to reduce its debt (Koo 2008, 2013). The Kaleckian algebra from Chapter 2 reveals that this reduction in private sector debt necessarily implies an increase in public sector debt, for Planet Earth if not for individual nations. Thus fiscal austerity will be self-defeating. If

$$\text{Expenditure} = C_w + C_p + I + G,$$

$$\text{Income} = W + P + T,$$

and there is no saving or dis-saving out of wages, so that

$$C_w = W,$$

Then

$$C_p + I + G = P + T,$$

and

$$G - T = P - (C_p + I),$$

so that the government's budget deficit $(G - T)$ must be equal to the private sector's surplus, the difference between capitalist income and capitalist expenditure $(P - C_p - I)$. Thus, when the private sector is intent on "de-leveraging" (that is, reducing its unacceptably high debt), an increase in government debt is part of the solution, not part of the problem. Any individual nation-state can run a trade surplus and thereby reduce both public and private sector debt, but this only increases the growth of public debt in its trading partners; it is not a solution for the world as a whole.

These are the "flow" equations. There is also a "stock" equation: if the government budget is in balance, so that $G = T$, the ratio of debt to income (D/Y) will rise or fall, depending on whether the rate of growth of national income (g) is less or greater than the rate of interest on the public debt (i). It follows that there are two ways of reducing D/Y: cut i or raise g. Conversely, even if the budget is in balance, there are two ways in which D/Y may rise: an increase in i and a reduction in g. These are the very simplest stock relations. They can be made more complicated by allowing for both budget deficits and austerity measures that succeed in the achievement of a budget surplus (Watts and Sharpe 2013). But the underlying principle remains: g and i are the two crucial variables that determine the course of D/Y over time. This has a direct bearing on the continuing crisis of the eurozone, and in particular the protracted depression in the PIIGS (Portugal, Ireland, Italy, Greece and Spain). This has been made much worse by the imposition of austerity, which has rendered g negative – hugely so in the case of Greece – while i remains positive (King 2015; Truger 2013).

The only good news in all of this is that a new GFC may be delayed, since successful de-leveraging in more fortunate countries does mean that the financial robustness of the private sector has increased; this is related to the "stock" aspect of Minsky's argument for "Big Government", outlined in the previous chapter. As the liberal Austrian journalist Josef Urschitz (2010) put it, the period 2007–09 saw the largest conversion of private debt into public debt in human history.

This, however, raises the bugbear of "fiscal sustainability". The precise meaning of this slippery concept remains unclear. One recent mainstream graduate text points to the importance of the private sector's willingness to hold government debt (Wickens 2008, pp. 96–104). If the debt–GDP ratio was expected to rise indefinitely, then concern that government would be unable to meet its debt obligations without having to resort to monetizing the debt, with the prospect of high and rising inflation (or even hyperinflation), might cause the private sector to be unwilling to hold government debt. The precise implications of this are, however, ambiguous. A necessary condition for fiscal sustainability is that the debt–GDP ratio is expected to remain finite. But this is an extremely weak condition, which is consistent with endless budget deficits and a debt–GDP ratio that rises continuously, though at a (very slowly?) declining rate. Similarly, Willem Buiter (2010) defines fiscal sustainability in Minskyian terms: it is necessary (and sufficient?) that the government avoids Ponzi finance, in which existing debt is serviced forever by issuing additional debt, so that the debt forever grows at least as fast as the interest rate on the debt. But this says nothing either about the ratio of debt to GDP or about the supposed virtues of stabilizing the debt–GDP ratio at any specific level. It is not an argument for austerity in the face of a deep recession.

If the debt–GDP ratio is considered to be a serious problem, for whatever reason, a case can be made for excavating the proposals for a progressive tax on capital, the so-called "capital levy", which were made by Ricardo in 1815 and by A.C. Pigou (1918) a century later, but never implemented. Similar suggestions were again made at the end of the Second World War, once more without success. A one-off 20 per cent wealth tax levied on the richest 10 per cent of the population would raise enough to pay off the United Kngdom's entire national debt (Philo 2010). A capital levy would ensure that the burden of reducing or eliminating the debt would fall on those best able to bear it, the rich, and not on those least able, the poor.

Even before the GFC the Japanese case had demonstrated that in a deep recession austerity only makes things worse, and that fiscal stimulus is the only effective remedy. However, measures to reduce income inequality should also be implemented. If the wage share were to rise at the expense of the profit share, and the top 1 per cent were to lose out to the bottom 99 per cent, there would be a boost to consumption expenditure and a reduction in unsustainable consumer debt. The precise macroeconomic consequences of an increase in the wage share depend on the values of the relevant parameters, and while for Planet Earth as a whole the prospects of a wage-led recovery seem good, and reduced inequality will bring significant macroeconomic benefits, it is unlikely to be enough to restore full employment (Onaran and Galanis 2012). Increased public expenditure – above all, investment in environmental improvements – will also be required.

There will also need to be improved international cooperation, to prevent the "new Mercantilism" that has allowed Germany and China to achieve large trade surpluses by screwing down wages. And the specific problems of the eurozone must be addressed. Even in 2015 the European Central Bank is a misnomer, since it lacks a coherent lender-of-last resort role and is thus unable to protect the integrity of the eurozone's financial system. There is also a strong case for a common European fiscal policy, though in the current populist–nationalist political climate it is difficult to see it coming any time soon (Hein 2012, chapter 8).

What have we learned? II: the need for de-financialization

The more intelligent use of fiscal policy is necessary to overcome the Great Recession and to reduce the likelihood of a new GFC, but it is not sufficient. In addition, a very substantial degree of de-financialization will be required to reduce the size, the instability and the political power of the global FIRE sector. This will entail a permanent reduction in the sector's share of GDP, aggregate profits and total employment, and also a qualitative transformation, replacing short-term profitability with a more balanced set of indicators of economic merit. In the wake of the GFC even shareholders may be prepared to accept this, up to a point, at least, since their interests lie in the long-term viability of the enterprise. But the interests of other stakeholders also need to be taken into account – customers, employees, local communities and the citizenry as a whole. Employee interests can be advanced through profit-sharing schemes, perhaps on the ambitious scale of the (never fully implemented) Swedish wage-earner funds that were proposed in the 1980s (Arestis 1986; Whyman 2006), and through the extension of the co-determination system that was once a significant constraint on the power of capital in large German companies. All these reforms will need to be bolstered by re-regulation of the labour market, to re-establish collective bargaining as the principal means of protecting wages and conditions of employment. And there will need to be a clear reversal of the privatization of housing and pensions that contributed to the financialization process in the neoliberal era.

There is substantial agreement among Post Keynesians about the detailed reforms that are required in the financial sector (King 2010; Wray 2013). In fact none of the regulatory weaknesses in the US financial system that were exposed by the GFC has been effectively addressed since 2007, and it is hard to disagree with Marc Jarsulic's conclusion that the potential for a disastrous future crisis remains, so long as there are still highly leveraged intermediaries dependent on short-term borrowing (Jarsulic 2013, p. 42).

The overriding principle of financial reform is the one established by Minsky: since financial innovation is ceaseless, financial regulators must be eternally vigilant, and regulations must be constantly reviewed and improved. Given this pre-condition, some specific suggestions follow. First, increased transparency: there must be no more off-balance sheet transactions, and the "sealed envelopes" full of securitized debts must be opened. Second, in order to ensure that this principle is applied in practice, there will need to be greatly enhanced regulation. A strong case can be made for the enforcement in the financial sector of the prudential principle that is operated by regulators in the pharmaceutical industry: no product should be authorized for sale unless it is both demonstrably safe *and* a clear need for it has been established (Tymoigne 2010).

Third, there need to be strong restrictions on speculation in commodities, especially by pension funds and other quasi-public financial institutions. Fourth, the behaviour of credit-rating agencies must be controlled, to remove the blatant conflict of interest that arises when these agencies are paid by the same corporations whose worthless securities they give "AAA" ratings to. Fifth, certain financial "products" should be eliminated altogether: Credit Default Swaps, to cite the most obvious example, should be outlawed, again because of the huge moral hazard issues that they raise. Sixth, central banks need additional instruments so that they can attack asset price bubbles without inflicting damage on output and employment by raising interest rates. Asset-based reserve requirements might be introduced, or direct quantitative controls over particular categories of lending, which were in widespread and generally successful use between 1939 and the early 1970s.

Internationally, a "new Bretton Woods" system would have to involve the release of the international financial institutions from the stranglehold of US and Western European financial interests, and the neoliberal ideology that they have imposed on poor countries must be replaced by a coherent policy programme designed to promote full employment and economic justice on a world scale. Serious consideration should be given to a return to the post-1945 system of fixed exchange rates, not because fluctuations in exchange rates may adversely affect the real economy through increased uncertainty that discourages investment (as argued by Davidson 2009), but rather because eliminating the private market in foreign exchange would greatly reduce the size of the financial sector. It is thus a key component of the de-financialization that is necessary if a new GFC is to be avoided.

Three final lessons

There are three final lessons to be drawn from the GFC (King 2011). First, the "neoliberal thought collective" that is represented by mainstream macroeconomics has proved itself to be very resilient indeed (Mirowski 2013). There is a great irony in this. If neoliberal policy precepts had actually been applied in the United States in late 2008, there would have been not a Great Recession but rather a repeat of the Great

Depression of 1929–33 – a genuine financial meltdown, together with a collapse in output and a rise in unemployment on a scale not seen since the early 1930s. If today there was 30 per cent unemployment in Germany and the United States it is unlikely that even the most charismatic and intellectually agile members of the thought collective would have continued to exert much influence.

The second lesson of the GFC concerns the continuing importance of the nation-state in an age of globalization. As argued by the Marxian theorist of imperialism, Ellen Meiskins Wood (2003), in an era of informal or "free market" imperialism, in which formal colonial rule is a thing of the past but US dominance survives, the other nation-states have a greater role to play than ever before in maintaining the global economic hierarchy. The truth of this proposition has been demonstrated both by the origins of the GFC and by the measures taken to overcome it.

Like the Great Depression, the GFC was indeed "made in the USA". This is not to deny that asset price bubbles, fraud, incompetence and systemic failure occurred elsewhere: the Northern Rock disaster in the United Kingdom and the nefarious activities of the Icelandic bankers, to name just two. But the crisis did not originate there, nor did it begin in some nebulous postmodern offshore non-location. It had a very specific and precisely defined site: Wall Street. The United States may be in decline as a political and military superpower, but it is still capable of initiating economic havoc and spreading it all over the world, just as it did in 1929. Once the GFC was underway, the international economic institutions were almost totally useless. Indeed, the International Monetary Fund was worse than useless, irrelevant to the larger national economies but inflicting savage and futile deflation on small and medium-sized countries. Effective measures to reduce the impact of the GFC came, as we have seen, from national governments, and from them alone. Thus globalization has not rendered the nation-state economically irrelevant or impotent. Quite the contrary: when the chips are down, there is still nothing else.

The final lesson concerns the limitations of neoliberalism, and in particular its fundamental precept: all social problems have a market solution, and where the relevant market does not yet exist it can and must be created (Howard and King 2008). This doctrine cannot in principle be applied to macroeconomics. Say's Law is false: supply does not create its own demand, and no market-mimicking arrangements can possibly eliminate the problem of effective demand. The truth of this statement was graphically revealed by the GFC and the reaction of nation-states to it. It is in no way affected by the allegedly inexorable march of globalization. In this sense, at least, Post Keynesians conclude, we still live in the world described by Keynes in the *General Theory*, three-quarters of a century ago.

References

Arestis, P. 1986. "Post Keynesian economic policies: the case of Sweden", *Journal of Economic Issues*, **20**(3), September, 709–23.

Arestis, P. and M. Sawyer. 2008. "A critical consideration of the foundations of monetary policy in the new consensus macroeconomic framework", *Cambridge Journal of Economics*, **32**(5), September, 761–79.

Barba, A. and M. Pivetti. 2009. "Rising household debt: its causes and macroeconomic implications – a long-period analysis", *Cambridge Journal of Economics*, **33**(1), January, 113–27.

Barberis, N. and. R. Thaler. 2003. "A survey of behavioral finance", in G.M. Constantindes, M. Harris and R.M. Stulz (eds), *Handbook of the Economics of Finance: Volume 1B: Financial Markets and Asset Pricing*, Amsterdam: Elsevier, pp. 1053–123.

Buiter, W.H. 2010. "The limits to fiscal stimulus", *Oxford Review of Economic Policy*, **26**(1), Spring, 48–70.

Dallery, T. 2009. "Post-Keynesian theory of the firm under financialization", *Review of Radical Political Economics*, **41**(4), Fall, 492–515.

Davidson, P. 2002. "Globalization", *Journal of Post Keynesian Economics*, **24**(3), Spring, 475–92.

Davidson, P. 2008. "Is the current financial distress caused by the subprime mortgage crisis a Minsky moment? Or is it the result of attempting to securitize illiquid non-commercial mortgage loans?", *Journal of Post Keynesian Economics*, **30**(4), Summer, 669–76.

Davidson, P. 2009. *The Keynes Solution: The Path to Global Economic Prosperity*, Basingstoke: Palgrave Macmillan.

Gabor, D. 2014. "The political economy of repo markets", Mimeo, University of Western England, Bristol.

Hein, E. 2012. *The Macroeconomics of Finance-dominated Capitalism – and Its Crisis*, Cheltenham, UK and Northampton, MA, USA: Edward Elgar.

Hein, E. and T. van Treeck. 2010. "Financialisation in Post-Keynesian models of distribution and growth – a systematic review", in M. Setterfield (ed.), *Handbook of Alternative Theories of Economic Growth*, Cheltenham, UK and Northampton, MA, USA: Edward Elgar, pp. 277–92.

Howard, M.C. and J.E. King. 2008. *The Rise of Neoliberalism in Advanced Capitalism: A Materialist Analysis*, Basingstoke: Palgrave Macmillan.

Jarsulic, M. 2013. "The origins of the US financial crisis of 2013", in M.H. Wolfson and G.A. Epstein (eds), *The Handbook of the Political Economy of Financial Crises*, Oxford: Oxford University Press, pp. 21–46.

Kapeller, J. and B. Schütz. 2014. "Debt, boom, bust: a theory of Minsky–Veblen cycles", *Journal of Post Keynesian Economics*, **36**(4), Summer, 781–814.

King, J.E. 2010. "Reflections on the global financial crisis", in S. Kates (ed.), *Macroeconomic Theory and Its Failings: Alternative Perspectives on the World Financial Crisis*, Cheltenham, UK and Northampton, MA, USA: Edward Elgar, pp. 143–58.

King, J.E. 2011. "Four theses on the global financial crisis", in S. Kates (ed.), *The Global Financial Crisis: What Have We Learned?*, Cheltenham, UK and Northampton, MA, USA: Edward Elgar, pp. 126–37.

King, J.E. 2015. "A Post Keynesian critique of Swabian housewife logic", in A. Bitzenis, N. Karagiannis and J. Marangos (eds), *Europe in Crisis*, Basingstoke: Palgrave Macmillan, pp. 29–43.

Koo, R. 2008. *The Holy Grail of Macroeconomics: Lessons from Japan's Great Recession*, Hoboken, NJ: John Wiley.

Koo, R. 2013. "Balance sheet recession as the 'other half' of macroeconomics", *European Journal of Economics and Economic Policies: Intervention*, **10**(2), 136–57.

Lazonick, W. 2013. "From innovation to financialization: how shareholder value ideology is destroying the US economy", in M.H. Wolfson and G.A. Epstein (eds), *The Handbook of the Political Economy of Financial Crises*, Oxford: Oxford University Press, pp. 491–511.

LiPuma, E. and B. Lee. 2004. *Financial Derivatives and the Globalisation of Risk*, Durham, NC: Duke University Press.

Minsky, H.P. 1987. "Securitization", Policy Note 2008/2, Levy Economics Institute of Bard College, Annadale-on-Hudson, NY.

Minsky, H.P. 1988. "Back from the brink", *Challenge*, **31**(1), January–February, 22–8.

Mirowski, P. 2013. *Never Let a Serious Crisis Go to Waste: How Neoliberalism Survived the Financial Meltdown*, London and New York: Verso.

Onaran, Ö. and G. Galanis. 2012. *Is Aggregate Demand Wage-led or Profit-led? National and Global Effects*, Geneva: International Labour Organization, Conditions of Work and Employment Series No. 40.

Palley, T. 2013. "Monetary policy and central banking after the crisis", in M.H. Wolfson and G.A. Epstein (eds), *The Handbook of the Political Economy of Financial Crises*, Oxford: Oxford University Press, pp. 624–43.

Philo, G. 2010. "It's time to tax the rich", *Guardian Weekly*, 20 August, p. 18.

Pigou, A.C. 1918. "A special levy to discharge war debt", *Economic Journal*, **28**(110), June, 135–56.

Silver, D. 2013. "Deregulation and the new financial architecture", in M.H. Wolfson and G.A. Epstein (eds), *The Handbook of the Political Economy of Financial Crises*, Oxford: Oxford University Press, pp. 430–46.

Stockhammer, E. 2013. "Financialization and the global economy", in M.H. Wolfson and G.A. Epstein (eds), *The Handbook of the Political Economy of Financial Crises*, Oxford: Oxford University Press, pp. 512–25.

Tobin, J. 1987. "On the efficiency of the financial system", in J. Tobin, *Policies for Prosperity: Essays in a Keynesian Mode*, Brighton: Wheatsheaf, pp. 282–96.

Truger, A. 2013. "Austerity in the euro area: the sad state of economic policy in Germany and the EU", *European Journal of Economics and Economic Policies: Intervention*, **10**(2), 158–74.

Turner, A. 2009. *The Turner Review: A Regulatory Response to the Global Banking Crisis*, London: Financial Services Authority.

Tymoigne, É. 2010. "The US mortgage crisis: subprime or systemic?", in G.N. Gregoriou (ed.), *Banking Crisis*, London: Taylor and Francis.

Urschitz, J. 2010. "Das hilflose Zappeln im Schuldennetz" ("Wriggling helplessly in the web of debt"), *Die Presse* (Vienna), leading article, 5 May, available at http://diepresse.co./meinung/kommentare/leitartikel/563097/print.do (accessed 6 May 2010).

Watts, M. and T. Sharpe. 2013. "Immutable laws of debt dynamics", *Journal of Post Keynesian Economics*, **36**(1), Fall, 59–84.

Whyman, P. 2006. "Post-Keynesianism, socialisation of investment and Swedish wage-earner funds", *Cambridge Journal of Economics*, **30**(1), February, 49–68.

Wickens, M. 2008. *Macroeconomic Theory: A Dynamic General Equilibrium Approach*, Princeton, NJ: Princeton University Press.

Wolfson, M.H. 2013. "An institutional theory of financial crises", in M.H. Wolfson and G.A. Epstein (eds), *The Handbook of the Political Economy of Financial Crises*, Oxford: Oxford University Press, pp. 172–90.

Wood, E. Meiskins. 2003. *Empire of Capital*, London: Verso.

Wray, L.R. 2009. "The rise and fall of money manager capitalism: a Minskian approach", *Cambridge Journal of Economics*, **33**(4), July, 807–28.

Wray, L.R. 2013. "A Minskyan road to financial reform", in M.H. Wolfson and G.A. Epstein (eds), *The Handbook of the Political Economy of Financial Crises*, Oxford: Oxford University Press, pp. 696–710.

9   Post Keynesians and other schools of thought

Orthodoxy and heterodoxy

There are evident similarities between Post Keynesians and a number of other heterodox (or quasi-heterodox) schools of thought. I discuss the relationships between them under four headings. The first three sections cover two such schools, which have something in common with each other: Marxian and Sraffian political economy; institutional and evolutionary economics; and feminist and ecological economics. Then I consider three schools that are themselves quite distinct, and can be seen either as an opportunity or as a threat: behavioural economics; complexity theory; and Austrian economics. I conclude with some reflections on the pluralist nature of Post Keynesianism itself.

The concept of heterodox economics is itself contested terrain. It implies the existence of a well-defined mainstream, to which all the various currents of heterodoxy are clearly opposed This has been contested on the grounds that orthodoxy has been fragmenting in recent years and is now effectively pluralist rather than monolithic, with non-neoclassical ideas from behavioural economics, complexity theory and evolutionary game theory, among quasi-heterodox streams of thought, constituting a new and very different analytical cutting edge (Davis 2008). There is an element of truth in this, but it is important not to exaggerate the decline of the mainstream, above all in macroeconomics, where the New Neoclassical Synthesis still reigns supreme.

There is also continuing controversy over the nature of heterodox economics itself. Fred Lee argues strongly that a single, coherent and more or less united heterodoxy is emerging. There are six heterodox traditions, he suggests – Post Keynesian–Sraffian, Marxist–radical, institutional–evolutionary, social, feminist and ecological economics – which together constitute a coherent alternative to mainstream economics. He insists that these are not multiple kinds of heterodox economics, but rather a single coherent alternative to the mainstream, since all six heterodox traditions emphasize factors such as accumulation, justice, social relationships in terms of class, gender and race, full employment and economic and social reproduction (Lee 2013).

I do not find this story very convincing, for the reasons set out in King (2013a). The best that can be said is that it represents a manifesto for the future development of heterodox economics (and one that I find very attractive). It is not, however, an accurate description of the status quo. In the remainder of this chapter I shall consider the relations between Post Keynesianism and five of Lee's heterodox schools, together with three that he does not mention: behavioural economics; complexity theory; and Austrian economics (of the von Mises–Hayek variety, not the Rothschild–Steindl version of Post Keynesian theory).

Marxian and Sraffian political economy

It is convenient to consider Marxian and Sraffian political economy together, since both have their intellectual origins in classical economics, above all the work of David Ricardo. It needs to be recognized at the outset that Marxian economics is itself a very diverse and sectarian movement. It does, however, have a lot in common with Post Keynesianism, especially, but not only, with its Kaleckian stream (Sardoni 1997). It deals explicitly with capitalist production, not (as is the case with much of mainstream macroeconomics) with exchanges between simple commodity producers. Marxists insist that economic theory must be historically and socially specific, changing with the different stages of capitalist development. Thus Marx distinguished the "manufacturing" and "modern industry" stages of early capitalism, Rudolf Hilferding identified a new stage of "finance capital" and Paul Baran and Paul Sweezy developed Lenin's notion of a late (and hopefully final) stage that they called "monopoly capital". As we saw in Chapter 6, Kaleckians also emphasize the significance of the differences between the competitive and monopoly stages of capitalism.

In the second and third volumes of *Capital* Marx began to develop a model of what Keynes would later term a "monetary production economy", revealing a common heritage that goes back to Quesnay and the very earliest models of the "circular flow" of income. It is easy to imagine that the later income–expenditure models representing a form of "hydraulic Keynesianism" might have appealed to Marx. As we have seen, in the 1933 draft of the *General Theory*, Keynes used Marx's

M-C-C'-M' model of the capitalist circulation process and followed rather closely the treatment of the "realisation problem" set out by Marx in volume II of *Capital* (Rotheim 1981).

Another common feature is that capitalists are the most important actors, not individual consumers or households, and business investment is the driving force in both the short run and the long run. In Marx's words: "accumulate, accumulate, this is Moses and the prophets". Marx and Keynes also share an emphasis on the instability of the capitalist system, focussing on its contradictions, its proneness to crisis and (in some versions of both schools) its tendency towards stagnation. And Marx was a strong critic of Say's Law.

But there are also some very substantial differences, above all on the question of policy prescriptions to save capitalism from itself. In part these reflect deeper problems of a political nature. Marxists tend to see Post Keynesians as apologists for capitalism, since they hope that capitalism can be made to work better and thus reject any tendency towards "fatalistic Marxism", according to which "the logic of capital" and the depth of the system's contradictions necessarily prevent any possibility of reform. Unlike Keynes, of course, Marx wanted to destroy the capitalist mode of production, not to rescue it.

In matters of detailed macroeconomic analysis, Marx's contribution should not be exaggerated. He wrote a lot about finance, but he did not produce a coherent theory of its role as a major source of economic crises. In any case, capitalism has moved on since his death, and as a firm advocate of historical specificity in the development of political economy he himself would have denied the relevance of *Capital* in explaining the details of a Global Financial Crisis that occurred almost a century and a half after he wrote it.

There are some further theoretical problems, which include the labour theory of value and the related issues of distinguishing productive from unproductive labour, determining what the "product" of labour actually is in a digital age and deciding whether there are still strong forces tending to equalize the rate of profit in a world of Schumpeterian temporary monopolies that are imperfectly protected by intellectual (rather than material) property rights. There are well-known difficulties with the theory of the falling rate of profit that Marx sketched in volume III of *Capital*, which are in turn related to several dichotomies – base/superstructure, production/circulation, real/monetary and underlying scientific reality/superficial appearances – none of which Post Keynesians would be at all comfortable with. Probably the most crucial problem in reconciling Marx and Keynes is the distinction between production and exchange, which Marx (and most of his followers) see as the most important instance of an even deeper dichotomy between underlying reality and superficial appearances. It is a dual that no Post Keynesian can accept.

The relationship between the Post Keynesians and Sraffian political economy is also a complicated one. As we have seen, Piero Sraffa himself played a major role in the early history of the Cambridge variant of Post Keynesianism, through the capital theory controversies and the critique of the marginal productivity theory of distribution. His disciples, especially Luigi Pasinetti, have developed growth models in a Sraffian vein in a conscious attempt to synthesize the two schools of thought. As late as 1988, Sraffian economics was seen as one of the three principal streams of Post Keynesian thinking, along with the fundamentalist Keynesians and the Kaleckians (Hamouda and Harcourt 1988). And there were indeed substantial areas of common ground, for example, in their emphasis on the analysis of a capitalist economy and on the role of the economic surplus.

By the late 1980s, though, there were already signs of growing tension between Sraffians and Post Keynesians, which had manifested themselves in a personal breach between Joan Robinson and Pierangelo Garegnani, and more generally in disharmony at the Trieste conferences where the two schools met and disagreed in the mid 1980s (King 2002, pp. 158–9). They have drifted further apart since then, so much so that a case can be made that they now represent two very different strands of heterodox economics, which are fundamentally inconsistent for a number of reasons.

This is in part a methodological problem. Sraffians stress the need to analyse "long period positions", which is difficult to reconcile with the Kaleckian view of the long run (set out in Chapter 6) as nothing more than a series of short runs. They appear to their critics to be engaged in the study of ergodic systems by means of closed system theorizing, and to ignore the Post Keynesian distinction between history and equilibrium. Thus they neglect the process of accumulation and concentrate on the less interesting question of comparisons of equilibrium positions, have nothing to say about path dependence and pay too much attention to rigour at the expense of realism. There is no role in

Sraffian models for fundamental uncertainty, money or the principle of effective demand; there are no agents, no entrepreneurs, no profit expectations, no financial constraints or financial instability (Hart and Kriesler 2014). Finally, since the relationship between the wage rate and the rate of profit in Sraffian models is monotonically declining, it is difficult (if not impossible) for their models to incorporate a "wage-led" growth regime.

However, a case can be made for a Post Keynesian–Sraffian synthesis. The Sraffians also reject Say's Law, but for a different reason: the relationship between relative input prices and the proportions in which the inputs are used in production is not necessarily monotonic, so that there is no guarantee that a reduction in real wages will lead to full employment. This is a different way of arriving at the principle of effective demand, but it is not inconsistent with Post Keynesian reasoning. In some ways, Heinz Kurz suggests, Sraffa went further than Keynes had been able to do in escaping from habitual, "classical" modes of thought in his rejection of the downward-sloping marginal efficiency of capital schedule, the liquidity preference theory of interest and exogenous nature of the money supply (Kurz 2013). This controversy is ongoing.

Institutionalism and evolutionary economics

Institutionalist and evolutionary economists share a common heritage in the work of Thorstein Veblen, and especially in his critique of the mechanical models used by "neoclassical" economists (a term that he invented). Veblen argued that rational calculation was less important than habit and custom in motivating economic behaviour, and that economics should base itself on evolutionary biology rather than on mechanics. By 1920 a distinct institutionalist school of economics had emerged in the United States, emphasizing the priority of empirical research – above all, the collection of data – over abstract theoretical work, and the importance for economic theory of collective action by the state and also by a range of voluntary associations, including corporations and trade unions (Rutherford 2011). The most prominent institutionalist of a later generation was John Kenneth Galbraith, who combined institutionalist and Keynesian themes in a series of influential books, in which he argued that the highly unionized, "Big Government", corporate capitalism of the post-1945 period was fundamentally different from the nineteenth-century owner-managed, competitive, liberal capitalist market system on which neoclassical economic theory was based, and therefore required a very different type of economic analysis.

Evidently there are some strong natural affinities between Post Keynesian and institutionalist thinking, beginning with an inter-disciplinary slant, since both schools have deep interests in the social and political foundations of economics. There is also a shared hostility to mainstream economics, in particular its formalism and especially its general equilibrium (and above all Dynamic Stochastic General Equilibrium) variants. There is a common emphasis on the role of habit, convention and the social influences on individual behaviour, along with an insistence on the importance of historical (rather than purely analytical) time, and the related phenomena of path dependence and cumulative causation. As we saw in Chapter 6, Post Keynesian growth theory pays a great deal of attention to the role of institutions, and especially institutional change, in the process of growth.

There is also considerable agreement on policy issues, since Post Keynesians and institutionalists tend to share a commitment to "Big Government" and a common heritage in the New Deal and the post-1945 social democratic compromise. This is especially apparent on the question of incomes policy, where the political and institutional aspects of inflation control are in the forefront, as we saw in Chapter 7 with the cooperation of the Post Keynesian Sidney Weintraub and the institutionalist Henry Wallich in the Tax-based Incomes Policy proposals of the early 1970s. Keynes himself was sympathetic to the institutionalism of his day, and there have been many later personal links; Fred Lee, Steve Pressman and Charles Whalen have been promi-nent in recent decades.

As we have seen, Galbraith and also Alfred Eichner had a large foot in both camps. Many Post Keynesians have published in the *Journal of Economic Issues*, and some institutionalists have also found a home for their work in the *Journal of Post Keynesian Economics* (Lee 2009, chapter 5). In 2013 a special issue of the *European Journal of Economics and Economic Policies* was devoted to the relationship between the two schools and the pros-pects for the creation of a single unified paradigm that draws on elements of both. "Broadly speaking", the editors suggested, "it could be argued that Institutionalism provides the microeconomics of this common paradigm, while post-Keynesian offers the macroeconomic framework" (Lavoie and Seccareccia 2013, p. 9). The institutionalists have much to say about labour markets, consumer theory, industrial organization, pricing and the theory of the firm, while Post Keynesians are stronger on the theory of employment, inflation, growth theory, international trade and finance, and monetary economics. "The last topic, theories of money and credit, is probably a good example of the benefits of combining an Institutionalist approach with post-Keynesian economics, since an appropriate knowledge of the mechanisms of monetary institutions, including those of the central bank, is critical in providing a relevant and realistic monetary theory" (p. 9).

On the negative side, institutionalists tend to be much less well disposed towards any formalism in theory or research methods, while Post Keynesians are suspicious of the "imperfectionist" element in institutionalist thought, exemplified by Gardiner Means's anti-Keynesian (or perhaps New Keynesian) interpretation of the Great Depression, which centred on price rigidity and made no reference to the principle of effective demand. To some extent this reflects the macroeconomic focus of the one and the microeconomic specialization of the other, and it could be argued that this offers a natural division of labour, with the Post Keynesians specializing on macroeconomics and formal theory, leaving micro issues and the socio-political background to the institutionalists. But this also points to some potential difficulties in the relationship. Unlike many institutionalists, few Post Keynesians are opposed in principle to formal modelling, so long as it is of the right type, or to the use of econometric methods, providing that they are used with the appropriate care and restraint. There are some important unresolved methodological tensions here.

Similarly, there is some disagreement between institutionalists and evolutionary economists on the question of formalism, which is almost always opposed by institutionalists but is often welcomed by evolutionary economists, who use game theory, the mathematics of complexity and large-scale computer simulation techniques in addition to verbal modes of argument. Evolutionary economists have a number of basic principles in common with Post Keynesians. First and foremost is the focus on change, not just in levels of output and in technology, but also in history, society and institutions. This has inspired the "evolutionary Keynesianism" and the predator–prey models of cyclical growth that were alluded to in Chapter 6.

Thus the two schools share a firm opposition to equilibrium modelling (or, at the very least, to static equilibrium modelling), and acceptance of the principles of path dependence, cumulative causation, emergent properties and hostility to explanation in terms of micro-reduction. There is also agreement on the central role of investment: even more than the institutionalists, evolutionary economists are conscious that they are dealing with a profit-driven capitalist economy, in which saving – and consumption – are secondary, and the profit expectations of entrepreneurs are crucial (Dopfer and Potts 2008). This emphasis on the implementation of innovation through investment is also a powerful theme in the work of Michał Kalecki, and suggests that the conclusions of the Kaleckian and evolutionary traditions can be integrated (Courvisanos 1996).

But it also points to some potential problems. Post Keynesians are suspicious of any temptation to glorify the entrepreneur, which is most obvious in the case of those evolutionary theorists most influenced by Joseph Schumpeter. They are concerned, too, by the tendency to confuse evolution – a process of random change, with no end goal and no guarantee of constant improvement – with economic and social progress, which involves steady improvement. Post Keynesians also worry about some evolutionary economists' tendency to see state failure as a bigger danger than market failure, and to deny that anything can be done about crises and instability, which perhaps reflects an anti-Keynesian perspective from which the economy is seen as supply-driven rather than demand-driven, involving hostility to macroeconomic reasoning and to the principle of effective demand. Thus it remains to be seen whether evolutionary and Post Keynesian economics are, after all, complementary projects.

Feminists and ecological economics

These two schools of thought have little in common other than the fact that they deal with aspects of economic life that Post Keynesians have tended to neglect. As we saw in Chapter 5, the role of gender and the household in microeconomics suggests that there is a degree of complementarity between feminism and Post Keynesianism, perhaps strengthened by the lack (thus far) of a specifically feminist theory of macroeconomics (van Staveren 2010, p. 1125), although feminists have begun to concern themselves with public finance, trade and financial markets. Feminists have, however, always taken a strong interest in the gender dimension to macroeconomic policy, and especially the impact of austerity on women, which seems to provide a very good example of the benefits from cooperation with Post Keynesians on policy questions.

Siobhan Austen and Therese Jefferson (2010) explore the connections between the two schools at the level of methodology. The similarities, they argue, are greater with respect to epistemology than they are on questions of ontology. The Post Keynesian call for pluralism clearly is consistent with feminist concerns, and is supported in both schools by acceptance of the complexity of social life and the openness of social systems. It might, perhaps, be broadened to include an explicit acceptance by Post Keynesians of a plurality of research methods to address specific research questions, which does follow from Sheila Dow's Babylonian approach to economic methodology (see Chapter 4).

Disagreement is more likely to arise over the Post Keynesian commitment to "realisticness" in theory construction, and thereby also to some form of scientific realism, which is difficult to reconcile with feminist emphasis (derived from postmodernist thought) on the androcentric nature of the modern philosophy of science, so that knowledge is regarded as a social construct. Austen and Jefferson (2010, p. 1113) quote Julie Nelson's list of desirable attributes for feminist economic theory: "Feelings! Emotions! Influence! Connection! Holism! Vagueness! Process! Value!" (Nelson 2003, p. 116). Post Keynesians would welcome some of these characteristics, but I suspect that they would be uncomfortable, to say the least, with several of them.

Irene van Staveren (2010, p. 1123) suggests that feminist economics is not a separate school of thought but rather a lens through which economic analysis is done, from a variety of – orthodox and heterodox – methodological approaches. Cross-fertilization with Post Keynesian theory is possible, she maintains, both on subjects that feminists have taken very seriously (gender, the household, unpaid work and caring labour) and those that they have tended to neglect (uncertainty, market power, endogenous dynamics). There is considerable common ground, with a shared belief that agents are socially embedded, a strong interest in the distribution of income and of welfare more broadly defined, and recognition of the role played by institutions in economic life. Van Staveren concludes that feminists and Post Keynesians can look forward to "a lively mutual learning process. Let's wish them a good journey together" (p. 1140). Or perhaps the most that can be expected is "productive discussion rather than ongoing cohabitation" (Austen and Jefferson 2010, p. 1119).

One or more of these metaphors might also be applied to the relationship between ecological economics and the Post Keynesians. As we saw in Chapter 7, there are significant areas of common ground on policy issues, and these might easily be extended to the domain of economic theory. One fundamental principle of ecological economics is the non-substitutability of natural and human-made capital, which fits rather well with the Post Keynesian inclination to downplay the role of substitution and instead to emphasize complementarities in both consumption and production. Equally, the ecologists could profit from an acceptance of some distinctively Post Keynesian principles, including the systemic nature of market failures and the need to establish social minimum standards to meet basic human needs, which might be extended from full employment and distributional equity to include environmental conditions. The Post Keynesian focus on production rather than exchange also lends itself to an ecological application, since pollution can be treated as an undesirable joint product, and the distinction between historical and analytical time points to the inevitable irreversibility of the use of raw materials and other natural resources (Perry 2013). As with feminism, a common journey with ecological economists appears to be highly desirable.

Behavioural economics, complexity and Austrian economics

The prospects for cohabitation with these three final heterodox (or quasi-heterodox) schools are rather less certain. There are indeed some obvious and important similarities between Post Keynesianism and behavioural economics, most obviously with the "Old Behaviouralism" of Herbert Simon and his associates (Jefferson and King 2010–11). Both schools reject the neoclassical conception of rationality, instead emphasizing the limits to human cognitive ability, the importance of fundamental uncertainty and the role of conventions and rules of thumb. There are also some points of agreement with "New Behaviouralism", most clearly on questions of the framing of decisions, the context of decision-making and what are sometimes described (unwisely, in my opinion) as the "macrofoundations" of individual behaviour.

These similarities have led Paul Davidson to describe Keynes as the first behavioural economist and Simon to claim him as the father of bounded rationality. But there is also a strong suspicion that the New Behavioural economics is really "neoclassical model building carried on by other means", as Simon once put it, and that it should therefore be avoided by Post Keynesians. It does seem that behavioural macroeconomics, which was foreshadowed by George Akerlof in his 2001 Nobel acceptance speech, is a promise that bounced. Akerlof and Shiller's book on *Animal Spirits* not only misinterprets Keynes on the prevalence of reasonable behaviour under conditions of fundamental uncertainty but also has almost nothing to say about investment or the investment–saving relationship (on all these matters, see King 2013b).

A slim volume by Paul de Grauwe (2012) demonstrates both the strengths and the weaknesses of behavioural macroeconomics. De Grauwe explicitly repudiates the assumption of rational expectations, on epistemological and ontological grounds. Agents have cognitive limitations, and therefore use rules of thumb because the real world is too complex for utility maximization. He abandons the representative agent, rejects Ricardian equivalence and instead asserts the effectiveness of fiscal policy. De Grauwe criticizes the mainstream advocacy of inflation targeting as the sole function of monetary policy, argues that central banks should also be responsible for some degree of output stabilization and maintains that asset price inflation should be of concern to the monetary authorities. His "behavioural business cycle" is endogenous, money is not neutral and the Phillips Curve is not vertical. There is a great deal here with which Post Keynesians will agree.

But the weaknesses are also evident. Although he is a strong critic of the standard DSGE model and especially of its RARE microfoundations, De Grauwe continues to use a standard three-equation model that is basically the same as the mainstream New Keynesian model. It yields the same results as the standard New Classical model when prices are perfectly flexible, so that counter-cyclical government policy is needed only because of price and wage rigidities. Like that of the New Classicals and New Keynesians, indeed, De Grauwe's is a strange sort of capitalist economy, with no workers or capitalists, no profits or wages, no employment or unemployment (though the existence of involuntary unemployment is presumably implicit in the concept of an output gap). Moreover, De Grauwe's "supply shocks" are confined to unexpected variations in productivity growth, since there is no space in the model for distributional conflict, wage-push inflation or fluctuations in primary product prices. He has nothing to say about financialization, the growth of debt, rising inequality in income and wealth or global imbalances, and it is difficult to see how his model could begin to get to grips with the continuing crisis of the eurozone.

Nevertheless, a case can be made for Post Keynesians making use of some aspects of behavioural economics, providing that it is done in a selective and self-critical way. This might allow a more realistic formulation of the investment function, which has always been a source of difficulty in Post Keynesian macroeconomics, and the behavioural finance literature may also be helpful to the Minskyans in their work on financial innovation and the challenges to financial regulation. There are also signs of a rediscovery of the work of George Katona (1980), whose ideas on consumer behaviour may well prove helpful in enabling a more accurate specification of the consumption function and thereby making one important part of the Post Keynesian macroeconomic model more realistic.

The implications of complexity economics are even more contentious. It must be noted at the start that the word "complexity" can be used in two rather different senses. Qualitatively, as employed, for example, by Kurt Rothschild, it forms an argument for pluralism and thus poses no problem for Post Keynesians. Quantitatively, as invoked by the endogenous money theorist Basil Moore (2006) and others, it is used as an argument against equilibrium modelling and for the use of complex dynamics (what used to be called "chaos theory"). On Moore's interpretation it has extremely damaging consequences for the equilibrium income–expenditure models used by all three of the Post Keynesian schools discussed in Chapter 2. All this has something in common with Paul Davidson's thinking on "non-ergodicity", but Davidson has always made extensive use of equilibrium analysis. It is also reminiscent of Kaldor's and Robinson's insistence on path dependence and the distinction between equilibrium and history, but they drew very different conclusions.

The critical issue, according to Moore, is that the "Keynesian multiplier" is inconsistent with endogenous money. But the multiplier is derived from the income–expenditure models that are central to all three Post Keynesian schools that were described in Chapter 2, which (if Moore is correct) must themselves be rejected. There are also large policy implications, as the fiscal and foreign trade multipliers must also be repudiated. Abandoning the investment–saving relationship would create a vast analytical hole, and very few Post Keynesians have been prepared to go this far, though a few, as we saw in Chapter 6, have used computer-simulated models of complex systems to model the process of cyclical growth. The broader issues remain largely unexplored. What might a complete "complexity–Post Keynesian" macroeconomic model look like? Since it would rely on agent-based modelling – constructing a "toy economy", as this is sometimes referred to disparagingly – would it still *be* macroeconomics? There seems to have been little or no systematic analysis by Post Keynesians of the methodological implications of agent-based modelling, leaving the nature of any future relationship with complexity economics undecided.

Finally, there are also some sharp points of difference between Austrian economists and the Post Keynesians, beginning with politics and methodology. The Austrians regard the state as part of the problem, not part of the solution, and they have no sympathy for the broadly social democratic position taken by most Post Keynesians. Their methodological individualism and subjectivism goes much too far for most Post Keynesians, sometimes leading them to deny the validity of macroeconomic theorizing of any sort.

But there is, again, some common ground, including a shared hostility to general equilibrium and to neoclassical theorizing more generally, and an acceptance of fundamental uncertainty and the role of historical time. This entails explicit rejection of certainty–equivalent utility- and profit-maximizing models, and an emphasis on the creative decision-making of the entrepreneur. The work of George Shackle (1955), which was dedicated to these questions, is sometimes seen as forming a bridge between the two traditions. And the Austrian insistence on the emergent properties of spontaneous economic evolution is difficult to reconcile with the micro-reduction principle that lies behind the "microfoundations" metaphor, again suggesting some common ground with the Post Keynesians.

When Austrians do engage in macroeconomic theorizing, however, the differences become apparent. While the investment–saving relationship is central to their analysis it is treated in a Wicksellian manner, with differences between the market rate of interest and the supposed "natural" rate given centre stage (Horwitz 2000). Not surprisingly, when in the 1980s the Austrian theorists Gerald O'Driscoll and Mario Rizzo tried to enlist Paul Davidson as an ally in their battle with the neoclassicals, he demurred. The Austrians, Davidson claimed, retained all three of the pre-Keynesian axioms that he rejected: neutral money, gross substitution and (more debatably) ergodocity (King 2002, pp. 230–33). Both before and after this brief exchange, Post Keynesians and Austrians have generally responded to what seem to be irreconcilable differences by simply ignoring each other.

Pluralism reconsidered

I began this chapter by referring to the contentious question of whether there was a single intellectual project known as "heterodox economics" that might pose a serious challenge to the mainstream. I shall end it by endorsing the rather less extreme position advanced by Edward Fullbrook, the founding editor of what used to be known as *Post-Autistic Economics Review* and is now *Real-World Economics Review*, one of the e-journals published by the World Economics Association established by Fullbrook and colleagues in 2011 (www.worldeconomicsassociation.org). Fullbrook maintains that non-neoclassical economists are at last beginning to come together for their own protection, on the basis of ten shared principles of a "New Political Economy" that distinguish it from the "Old Political Economy" that they all reject (Rosenberg 2014).

These ten principles are (1) the need for pluralism; (2) the ontology of much economic phenomena does not lend itself to formal modelling and mathematical deduction; (3) economic analysis should be reality-based, not model-based; (4) non-equilibrium rather than equilibrium thinking; (5) non-market clearing rather than market clearing; (6) denial of stable preferences and rational, maximizing behaviour; (7) emergent properties, which make micro-reduction impossible and the microfoundations metaphor inapplicable; (8) non-ergodicity; (9) the economy is a subset of the planet, and not vice versa; and (10) a sharp distinction between positive and normative statements cannot be maintained. These principles, Fullbrook maintains, were all acknowledged in the "pluralist revolution" that took place in the natural sciences in the early twentieth century, but they have yet to reach mainstream economics. Perhaps they offer a formula for long-term cooperation between Post Keynesians and most, if not all, of the other heterodox tendencies that have been discussed in this chapter.

References

Akerlof, G. and R. Shiller. 2009. *Animal Spirits: How Human Psychology Drives the Economy, and Why It Matters for Global Capitalism*, Princeton, NJ: Princeton University Press.

Austen, S. and T. Jefferson. 2010. "Feminist and post-Keynesian economics: challenges and opportunities", *Cambridge Journal of Economics*, **34**(6), November, 1109–22.

Courvisanos, J. 1996. *Investment Cycles in Capitalist Economies: A Kaleckian Behavioural Contribution*, Cheltenham, UK and Brookfield, VT, USA: Edward Elgar.

Davis, J.B. 2008. "The turn in recent economics and the return of orthodoxy", *Cambridge Journal of Economics*, **32**(3), May, 349–66.

De Grauwe, P. 2012. *Lectures on Behavioral Macroeconomics*, Princeton, NJ: Princeton University Press.

Dopfer, K. and J. Potts. 2008. *The General Theory of Economic Evolution*, London and New York: Routledge.

Hamouda, O.F. and G.C. Harcourt. 1988. "Post Keynesianism: from criticism to coherence", *Bulletin of Economic Research*, **40**(1), January, 1–33.

Hart, N. and P. Kriesler. 2014. "Keynes, Kalecki, Sraffa: coherence?", Mimeo, University of New South Wales.

Horwitz, S. 2000. *Microfoundations and Macroeconomics: An Austrian Perspective*, London and New York: Routledge.

Jefferson, T. and J.E. King. 2010–2011. "Can Post Keynesians make better use of behavioral economics?", *Journal of Post Keynesian Economics*, **33**(2), Winter, 211–34.

Katona, G. 1980. *Essays on Behavioral Economics*, Ann Arbor, MI: Institute for Social Research, University of Michigan.

King, J.E. 2002. *A History of Post Keynesian Economics since 1936*, Cheltenham, UK and Northampton, MA, USA: Edward Elgar.

King, J.E. 2013a. "Post Keynesians and others", in F.S. Lee and M. Lavoie (eds), *In Defense of Post-Keynesian and Heterodox Economics: Response to Their Critics*, London and New York: Routledge, pp. 1–17.

King, J.E. 2013b. "Should post-Keynesians make a behavioural turn?", *European Journal of Economics and Economic Policies: Intervention*, **10**(2), 231–42.

Kurz, H. 2013. "Sraffa, Keynes, and Post-Keynesianism", in G.C. Harcourt and P. Kriesler (eds), *The Oxford Handbook of Post-Keynesian Economics, Volume 1: Theory and Origins*, Oxford: Oxford University Press, pp. 51–73.

Lavoie, M. and M. Seccareccia. 2013. "Editorial to the special issue", *European Journal of Economics and Economic Policies: Intervention*, **10**(1), 8–11.

Lee, F.S. 2009. *A History of Heterodox Economics: Challenging the Mainstream in the Twentieth Century*, London and New York: Routledge.

Lee, F.S. 2013. "Heterodox economics and its critics", in F.S. Lee and M. Lavoie (eds), *In Defense of Post-Keynesian and Heterodox Economics: Response to Their Critics*, London and New York: Routledge, pp. 104–32.

Moore, B.J. 2006. *Shaking the Invisible Hand: Complexity, Endogenous Money and Exogenous Interest Rates*, Basingstoke: Palgrave Macmillan.

Nelson, J. 2003. "Once more with feeling: feminist economics and the ontological question", *Feminist Economics*, **9**(1), 109–18.

Perry, N. 2013. "Environmental economics and policy", in G.C. Harcourt and P. Kriesler (eds), *The Oxford Handbook of Post-Keynesian Economics, Volume 2: Critiques and Methodology*, Oxford: Oxford University Press, pp. 391–411.

Rosenberg, P. 2014. "New Paradigm Economics versus Old Paradigm Economics. Interview with Edward Fullbrook", *Real-World Economics Review*, **66**, 13 January,

131–43, available at http://rwer.paecon.net/PAEReview/issue66/Fulbrook66.pdf (accessed 22 December 2014).

Rotheim, R. 1981. "Keynes's monetary theory of value (1933)", *Journal of Post Keynesian Economics*, **3**(4), Summer, 568–85.

Rutherford, M. 2011. *The Institutionalist Movement in American Economics, 1918–1947*, Cambridge: Cambridge University Press.

Sardoni, C. 1997. "Keynes and Marx", in G.C. Harcourt and P. Riach (eds), *A "Second Edition" of the General Theory, Volume 2*, London: Routledge, pp. 261–83.

Shackle, G.L.S. 1955. *Uncertainty in Economics and Other Reflections*, Cambridge: Cambridge University Press.

Van Staveren, I. 2010. "Post-Keynesianism meets feminist economics", *Cambridge Journal of Economics*, **34**(6), November, 1123–44.

10 Some final questions

Does Post Keynesian economics have a future? If so, what might that future look like? I asked these questions at the very beginning of the new century (King 2002, pp. 255–60). Four possibilities needed to be considered, I suggested. The first was migration out of economics into other social science departments within academia, and to research institutes outside the university system. Second, Post Keynesians might be absorbed painlessly back into the mainstream of academic economics, having made their point and having seen some of their theoretical positions and policy proposals accepted. Third, they might be incorporated into a broader body of heterodox economics, a process that some observers claimed to be already under way. Finally, they might survive as an embattled minority. I concluded that this fourth outcome was the most likely medium-term prospect, and on this, at least, I was not wrong.

In some ways the sense of being under siege is even stronger among Post Keynesians today, at least in the English-speaking world. The damage done to heterodox economics of all varieties by the UK's Research Assessment Exercise has been documented by Fred Lee (2009, chapters 8–9). In Australia a journal ranking exercise that eliminated all non-mainstream journals other than the *Cambridge Journal of Economics* from the "A*" and "A" categories has made mere survival an increasingly ambitious target for the relatively few remaining Post Keynesians. Less blatant but in the long term probably equally insidious processes are at work in Canada and the United States. In all these countries the increased power of university managers is undermining academic freedom, posing a severe threat to what is left of pluralism in economics. In several European countries, too, Post Keynesian economics is becoming collateral damage in other people's intellectual and managerial wars.

But things do seem to be appreciably worse in economics. There is no single, intolerant, monolithic mainstream in anthropology, economic geography, psychology, political science or sociology (Backhouse and Fontaine 2010). As an earlier volume in Elgar's "Advanced Introduction" series has demonstrated, in the discipline of international political economy the extent of paradigmatic diversity is breathtaking (Cohen 2014). Why *is* economics the only social science with an intolerant and monolithic mainstream? What might be done about it?

I have been asking myself these questions for many years, and I am still not convinced that I have the answers (indeed, there may *be* no answer to the second question). Physics envy is almost certainly part of the answer to the first question: real science demands equations, or so mainstream economists believe, and in macroeconomics these equations must set out a Dynamic Stochastic General Equilibrium model. Post Keynesian "theory" is simply not scientific economics. There is, of course, also a policy – and therefore a political – dimension. As we saw in Chapter 8, immensely powerful vested interests made good use of the Capital Asset Pricing Model and the efficient markets hypothesis to have financial regulation greatly weakened and their own profits (in the short term, at least) greatly increased. And the pernicious phenomenon of regulatory capture applies to central bankers as much as to industry regulators. It suits all parties – hedge fund managers, mainstream economists, central bankers – to dismiss dissenting opinions on money and on monetary policy as "not proper economics".

In these circumstances the migration strategy for Post Keynesians might need to be reconsidered. They would certainly be well advised to cultivate links with the other social sciences, and to collaborate more than they do at present with scholars working in other disciplines. Some have already found a home in departments of public policy, international political economy, politics and sociology, and some even (taking a very deep breath) in business schools. However, multidisciplinarity does come at a cost, given the difficulties in communication that are entailed by the very different backgrounds, paradigms and theoretical languages of scholars in different academic disciplines, and it would be sensible to think about the alternatives.

One such is advocated by Tim Thornton (2013) on the basis of the very successful experience, now extending over several decades, of the department of political economy at the University of Sydney (Butler et al. 2009). Thornton urges the "social science wing" of economics to constitute itself as a separate, independent discipline of "political economy" within faculties of social science. Post Keynesians would, of course, feel very much at home as representatives of such a discipline. Failing that, they will need to find other ways of reproducing themselves, in particular by making Post Keynesian themes a central part of their teaching inside mainstream economics departments (see Lavoie 2013 for a very constructive and illuminating Canadian case study). In the process they will profit from contact with the International Confederation of Associations for Pluralism in Economics (www.icape. org).

It would be wrong to end on too pessimistic a note. Students themselves are not universally satisfied with the current state of mainstream economics. Echoing the earlier complaints of the French students who established the Post-Autistic Economics movement (Fullbrook 2003), in late 2013 the Post-Crash Economics Society at the University of Manchester began to campaign for reform of their own unduly narrow economics syllabus. By mid 2014 there was a thriving International Student Initiative for Pluralism in Economics (ISIPE), bringing together 42 university economics associations in 19 countries, from Australia to Uruguay, and calling for the introduction of theoretical, methodological and inter-disciplinary pluralism into the core of the economics curriculum (www.isipe.net).

By their nature student movements tend to be short-lived, since being a student is itself a transient state. At the time of writing, however (December 2014), ISIPE seems to offer real hope for the future of heterodox economics in general, and for Post Keynesianism as a substantial component part of this heterodoxy.

References

Backhouse, R.E. and P. Fontaine (eds). 2010. *The History of the Social Sciences since 1945*, Cambridge: Cambridge University Press.

Butler, G., E. Jones and F. Stilwell (eds). 2009. *Political Economy Now! The Struggle for Alternative Economics at the University of Sydney*, Sydney: Darlington Press.

Cohen, B.J. 2014. *Advanced Introduction to International Political Economy*, Cheltenham, UK and Northampton, MA, USA: Edward Elgar.

Fullbrook, E. (ed.). 2003. *The Crisis in Economics: The Post-autistic Economics Movement: The First 600 Days*, London: Routledge.

King, J.E. 2002. *A History of Post Keynesian Economics since 1936*, Cheltenham, UK and Northampton, MA, USA: Edward Elgar.

Lavoie, M. 2013. "Teaching post-Keynesian economics in a mainstream department", in J. Jespersen (ed.), *Teaching Post Keynesian Economics*, Cheltenham, UK and Northampton, MA, USA: Edward Elgar, pp. 12–33.

Lee, F.S. 2009. *A History of Heterodox Economics: Challenging the Mainstream in the Twentieth Century*, London and New York: Routledge.

Thornton, T. 2013. "The narrowing of the Australian university economics curriculum: an analysis of the problem and a proposed solution", *Economic Record*, **89**(S1), June, 106–14.

Index